Not All Poor People Are Black

and other things we need to think more about

Not All Poor People Are Black

*and other things
we need to* think *more about*

Essays by

Janet Cheatham Bell

SABAYT
PUBLICATIONS

Not All Poor People Are Black

and other things
we need to think *more about*

Some of the essays in the electronic version of this book include Internet links. In the hard copy the URL's for these links are at the end of each essay, and are indicated by **boldface** in the text.

For reprint permission or to purchase copies, contact the author at www.janetcheathambell.com.

ISBN: 978-0-9616649-7-8

Second Printing, 2016

Book and cover design by Merridee LaMantia

Belmantia Publishing Services
BelmantiaPublishing@gmail.com

To the American people who are
the final reservoir of power.

For all those who want more from themselves and
more from their country.

West African Adinkra symbol
of unity and human relations.

A reminder to contribute to the community;
that in unity lies strength.

In memory of Julian Bond (1940-2015)
He did his part.

ACKNOWLEDGMENTS

I AM GRATEFUL TO HAVE RECEIVED HELP from a number of people during the years I've been occasionally writing these essays. The members of Bloomington's Our Writing League (OWL) gave me valuable feedback when I participated in that group. Vinita Moch Ricks, D. Delores Logan and Jennifer Deam not only read and offer suggestions on how to improve my writing, but as dear friends, they support, encourage and sustain me. I am also supported by Wild at Heart and the Friday Reading Group. My home girl and kindred spirit A'Lelia Bundles regularly provides the incentive a writer needs, even when not aware she's doing so. Ursula McPike, who was my intern when I started my career in book publishing, has developed into a top-notch wordsmith. Over the years, she has offered her editorial expertise to help me with my work and she continues to do so. My son Kamau is my trusted advisor and ardent cheerleader. He always tells me the unvarnished truth, and makes sure I am up-to-date on the latest electronic devices and social media. I am also nurtured by the rest of my family, Melissa, Sami, Denise, Tony, Kevin, Michael, Gregory, Miguel, Madganna, Regina, Kym and Natasha.

I gratefully give a shout-out to Maryellen May Greulich. Not only did her Transparent Works film my fabulous videos, but she held my hand throughout the twists and turns of the Kickstarter campaign. I have a new collaborator and friend! And gratitude as well to my Kickstarter supporters. Although I didn't reach the goal I set, your willingness to back my project kept my spirit soaring. Most of all, I give thanks to the off-line donors without whom the publication of this book may have been postponed indefinitely.

CONTENTS

What This Book is About

The Final Reservoir of Power x
The American people are the final reservoir of power.

Discovering **Personal Power**

Embracing Compassion 2
Our task must be to free ourselves by widening our circle of compassion.

Choosing a Life in the Dark Age 3
You make what seems a simple choice.

Expanding Possibilities 12
In every moment of our existence, we are in that field of all possibilities.

For Love of a Child: My Journey to Health 25
Until you've had a child you're just guessing about love.

Remembering Daddy 32
It doesn't matter who my father was; it matters who I remember he was.

Never Failing to Protest 40
There may be times when we are powerless to prevent injustice.

Making Changes, Being Changed 51
All that you touch, You Change.

Writing for Myself and Hoping 63
*Better to write for yourself and have no public, than to write for
the public and have no self.*

Looking Forward with Aging Grace 67
No matter how old you are there's always something good to look forward to.

Seeking **Spiritual Power**

Looking for God..**74**
*The nature of God is a circle of which the center is everywhere
and the circumference is nowhere.*

Spirituality and Organized Religion **79**
*The whole point in being alive is to evolve into the
complete person you were intended to be.*

Using My Consciousness...**84**
*Most people live, whether physically, intellectually or morally,
in a very restricted circle.*

Immortality: Beyond Marble or Monuments................**89**
*Not marble, nor the gilded monuments
Of princes, shall outlive this powerful rhyme.*

Using **Communal Power**

The Big White Lie: America's Racial Paradigm................**92**
The pervasive violence in our society is rooted in the paradigm of race.

The Viewer's Involvement **99**
The work itself has a complete circle of meaning and counterpoint.

The Help: How to Comfort Whites **103**
If you look for truth, you may in the end find comfort.

Living History: Movies About Slavery **107**
The plain truth is that slavery was an unprecedented economic juggernaut.

Letting My Peaches Go..**111**
Resentment is like taking poison and waiting for the other person to die.

Rules for Women Who Can't Do Enough........................**121**
*No woman can control her destiny if she doesn't give to herself
as much as she gives of herself.*

Speaking Out for Mass Transit................................133
*We don't all have the ability to sing out over a racing train,
but we do have the power to speak.*

Economics and the Ecosystem: A Lament................................140
Real tragedy is never resolved; it goes on hopelessly forever.

Shelby Steele: A Bound Man................................145
Dogma draws a circle round the mind.

**The Wit to Win: Oprah and the POTUS,
Pragmatic or Authentic?**................................148
He drew a circle that shut me out—Heretic, rebel, a thing to flout.

**Not All Black People Are Poor;
Not All Poor People are Black**................................156
*Emancipate yourselves from mental slavery; none but ourselves
can free our minds.*

Index................................166

Books by Janet Cheatham Bell................................179

About the Author................................180

About the Designer................................180

WHAT THIS BOOK IS ABOUT
The Final Reservoir of Power

To the American people who are the final reservoir of power in this country and whose values and expectations set the limits for those who exercise authority.

~ "Speak Truth to Power: A Quaker Search
for an Alternative to Violence"

"TOO BIG TO FAIL" IS THE MOST ridiculous assertion ever uttered. It contradicts every wisdom tradition and universal law understood or experienced by humanity. Michael Jordan made a more judicious statement about failure when he said, "I've failed over and over and over again; and that is why I succeed." Everybody fails at something at some point. It is because we make mistakes and learn the lessons of failure that we grow. Then we go on to fail again and learn more. **Nassim Taleb** calls this "antifragility." In his book, *Antifragile: Things That Gain from Disorder*, he says, "We have been fragilizing the economy, our health, political life, education, almost everything." In other words, we should be willing to explore the unknown and, through trial and error, discover unpredictable possibilities. Instead, we make monumental efforts to control the outcomes of the economy, politics, education, and relationships. Yet, we still cannot prevent the unanticipated. (Did anybody besides Barack Obama expect him to be elected president in 2008?) We spend billions on insurance to protect ourselves while insurance companies offer bonuses to employees who figure out how to avoid paying justifiable claims. We should welcome and learn from the unexpected rather than being devastated and demanding that things remain the same.

Even the United States of America is not too big to fail. This country made a mistake in going to war in Vietnam. From that our politicians learned that if you're going to fight an unpopular war, do it with volunteer troops rather than drafting people into the military. With our current, allegedly-winding-down wars in Iraq and Afghanistan, which are also mistakes, the country is discovering the devastation wreaked by repeated deployment of an all-volunteer army. Not only does it affect the nation's long-term mental, emotional, physical and economic well-being, but members of the armed forces and their families can be permanently wrecked by it. Perhaps the country's next lesson will be that going to war has no upside. One can only hope. However, as I write this, the disruption of Iraq's sovereignty initiated by the Bush administration in 2002 has flared into civil war there. And the same folk who told whopping lies to get support for that invasion are now insisting that the U.S. send more troops to Iraq. Their bare-faced audacity is astounding. Apparently their driving motivation, to the exclusion of the country's and our military's well-being, is to keep the **billions of dollars flowing** from the U.S. government to privately-owned war industries like Halliburton's KBR, which apparently has pocketed more than $39 billion from the American presence in Iraq.

This collection of essays is about identifying and using the power we have as members of the American body politic to work together for our *common good*. The essays also emphasize our mutual dependency. Standing aside to criticize and assign blame is to avoid loving and caring for yourself and others. We are enclosed in this circle of life *together* and need each other; we need to live in community, whether we acknowledge it or not.

The first nine essays are largely autobiographical as I write about some life experiences that helped me discover my own power. The second section consists of four essays about religion and spirituality that discuss my search for a satisfying spiritual life. The final eleven essays cover a range of topics that impact our interactions with one another in the public sphere: the environment, economics, entertainment, mass transit, politics, and race relations. It concludes with the title essay. The essays may be read in any order because each one is complete and stands on its own.

Many of the essays reflect my effort to make sense of the world I inhabit, which I do by writing about what I observe and experience. Some ruminations were originally blog entries on subjects that annoyed me at the time. One is an excerpt of a chapter from my memoir-in-progress. I depart from "conventional wisdom" on some issues because I want to provoke readers to consider these topics from another angle.

I've observed that, despite our alleged belief in rugged individualism, many Americans behave as if we deserve a life of certainty, a life without problems or significant ups and downs. And when bad things happen, we demand that our elected officials "do something!" We want instant solutions to every challenge, no matter how complicated or difficult. If a coach hasn't quickly produced a winning team, he's fired. If the economy doesn't improve instantly, approval ratings for the President plummet. When a catastrophe occurs—oil spill, hurricane, disappearance of an airplane—we become angry and frustrated with officials for not having prevented or prepared for the unforeseen disaster. In the words of blues singer Keb' Mo', we have become **"Victims of Comfort."** Our governments—local, state and particularly national—feed this delusion. When prices continue to rise on everything except the income of workers; it is called "economic growth." Obviously, the economic prognosticators see no difference between inflation and increased value. We are told, and many apparently believe, that when the stock market goes up, wealth will eventually "trickle down" to benefit us all. The chairman of the Federal Reserve Bank constantly "fixes" the economy by bailing out financial institutions, moving interest rates up and down, or removing them altogether for those who are at the top of the monetary food chain. Much of the time these economic "experts" have no idea what they are doing, but when we become uncomfortable, we insist that things be restored as they were. Because we demand not to be inconvenienced, politicians have learned to *talk* a good game. They get elected by promising to "create jobs," but do so only if that means favorable consideration and tax breaks for their corporate donors. We complain bitterly about this, but consistently re-elect the same state and national representatives no matter how many times they fail to deliver as promised.

Also because of our fragility, elected officials pretend that wars can be fought without collective consequences and sacrifices. As a result, we patriotically laud the troops, but do not pay them well—some families have to seek public assistance. After repeated deployments, service members return home to be mistreated and forgotten until Memorial Day and Veterans' Day.

Let's tell it like it is. The banks, insurance companies and other financial institutions did, in fact, fail. Big Time. "Too big to fail" was a euphemism coined to disguise the truth, which was that these institutions were *too powerful and politically connected to experience the consequences of their failure.* And where did this power come from? It came from U.S. citizens! The people we elected to office used our tax revenue to make sure that the failed financial institutions could continue the same policies and procedures. And because we bailed them out; these failed institutions *learned nothing.* Of course they will fail again. The question is: will we allow them to avoid the consequences of their behavior again? Because it is up to us. We are the final reservoir of power.

We are responsible to think for ourselves. In the words of **Howard Schultz**, CEO of Starbucks, Inc., "We can't wait for Washington. We have to step up, as we've done in the past, and demonstrate true leadership." Each of us is responsible to hold accountable the officials we elect to manage the country. We can organize to challenge politicians who refuse to represent our interests. We can become active in our communities, write, speak out, and above all, vote our preferences. And we have proof that our votes count; otherwise there would not be such bold and unconstitutional laws being passed to make voting more difficult, if not impossible, for certain groups of citizens. **Charles Blow**, *New York Times* columnist, says, "Voter apathy is a civic abdication. There is no other way to describe it." I absolutely agree. Each of us is culpable for the world we inhabit. So long as we believe we do not have the ability to respond to our life challenges and, instead, wait for political leaders to rescue us, we will continue to flail about in confusion, bobbing from one economic crisis or "recession" to the next. By accepting the reality of the world, we acknowledge that things inevitably and inexorably change. When changes occur, rather than insisting that elected officials "do something" to give the appearance of returning things to the way they were, we must prepare for a new order. Much of this carping is driven by the proliferation of media outlets, each striving for attention, which encourages these media to stir the pot and create drama where none exists.

I have long thought we should be more creative about our work lives, so I was delighted to read the article **"Is It Possible to Build an Economy Without Jobs?"** by Frank Joyce, president of the Michigan Coalition for Human Rights. Joyce says, "Humans will always work. But that whole employee-employer thing is optional. It's time to start looking for another model."

I agree with Joyce that we need to find a new model. My idea is to encourage and support the entrepreneurial spirit. The "handyman" who cleans out your gutters and mows your lawn is an entrepreneur. The woman you hire to look after your children is an entrepreneur. The homeless person who collects aluminum cans to be sold for recycling is an entrepreneur. The "scrapper" who plunders abandoned buildings for metal is an entrepreneur. The self-employed writer, graphic designer, interior designer, performer, caterer are all entrepreneurs. Such endeavors sometimes lead to hiring others to help with the work, but they may not. I define an entrepreneur as any person who takes charge of his/her own life by doing something that needs doing and making a living in the process. **Ameena Matthews**, Violence Interrupter in Chicago, is a prime example of such a person. We are all capable of being entrepreneurs. However, too many get stuck on the notion that being an entrepreneur means following the *Shark Tank* model: writing a business plan, convincing a venture capitalist to invest in the idea, then starting a national "business" that hires employees. That's one way to proceed, but not the only way.

The Internet has helped to level this playing field as it has many others. (As I write this, however, greedy corporations are using their political clout to end **net neutrality.** It is up to us to make our voices heard to prevent that from happening.) Crowd funding is becoming increasingly popular and is a more democratic way to raise varying amounts of money to finance innovative ideas. The plant researcher Sally Fox, who bred and grew naturally colored cotton that did not need to be dyed, turned to **crowd funding** to get that project going again. Also in the homegrown textile industry, **Fibershed,** in California "brings the farmers and artisans of [the] region together to provide [customers] with both raw fibers and finished goods that represent the fusion and artistry of the community." However the business evolves, an entrepreneur earns a living while also helping others.

Working together we all triumph, but if we continue to rage at each other over life's inevitable ups and downs, we will prolong the destructive bitterness and anger of our current economic/political/social malaise.

In the 1960s when people came together to dismantle racial segregation and express our abhorrence for the Vietnam War, we had a chant: THE PEOPLE UNITED, CANNOT BE DEFEATED. Reviving that sentiment are the Occupy movement, the anti-fracking movement in Colorado, the fast-food workers demanding a higher minimum wage, the football players at Northwestern

University, the DREAMers in the nation's capital insisting on immigration reform, the Moral Monday demonstrators opposing some Southern state governments' moves to restrict voting rights, and the Black Lives Matter movement. It is still *up to us*. We are the final reservoir of power.

Links:

Nassim Taleb http://www.nytimes.com/2012/12/17/books/antifragile-by-nassim-nicholas-taleb.html?pagewanted=all

billions of dollars flowing http://readersupportednews.org/news-section2/308-12/16561-focus-cheneys-halliburton-made-395-billion-on-iraq-war

Victims of Comfort *http://www.lyricsmode.com/lyrics/k/keb_mo/victims_of_comfort.html*

Howard Schultz *Daily Show with Jon Stewart*, June 16, 2014 http://thedailyshow.cc.com/videos/4lqlz1/howard-schultz

Charles Blow "We Should Be in a Rage" http://www.nytimes.com/2014/04/10/opinion/blow-we-should-be-in-a-rage.html?hp&rref=opinion&_r=0

Build an Economy Without Jobs http://www.alternet.org/story/155186/is_it_possible_to_build_an_economy_without_jobs?page=0%2C0

Ameena Matthews http://www.huffingtonpost.com/2012/02/02/ameena-matthews-the-interrupters_n_1250150.html

net neutrality http://www.latimes.com/business/hiltzik/la-fi-mh-murder-of-net-neutrality-20140429,0,3234289.column#axzz30QhTycPl

crowd funding
http://www.indiegogo.com/projects/help-me-grow-my-cotton-again

California Fibershed http://www.fibershed.com/

★ ★ ★

Discovering

Personal Power

᚛ Embracing Compassion

*Our task must be to free ourselves . . .by widening our
circle of compassion to embrace all living creatures and the
whole of nature and its beauty.*

~ Albert Einstein

I HAD AN EXCHANGE with a friend that may change my life.

He said as a Buddhist he learned that every action is an act of
LOVE OR FEAR.

I thought about this for a few minutes and I got it! He's
exactly right. I am no longer bothered when people pejoratively
call me "nigger," because I don't fear that word. At one point in
our history, racist bigots were free to terrorize their victims with
impunity, and often with the tacit or explicit legal support of
their communities and governments. The George Zimmermans
of America notwithstanding, over the years new legislation and a
shift in most American attitudes have made it possible for black
Americans to have some protection from the random racist acts
of the past.

There are currently many racist and fear-based myths being
repeated *ad infinitum* in the media and on the Internet. I've often
been annoyed, even infuriated, when I've encountered these
hateful myths, but this is a waste of my energy. The people who
traffic in invective are merely wailing about their fear of a changing world—a fear generated largely by their inability to halt the
changes. Neither they nor the notions they're spouting can harm
me, so I will consider these frightened people with compassion. Perhaps their personal life experiences have driven them
to interpret the world with fear and loathing. However, if I don't
resist or respond to hateful messages, I preserve and expand love
rather than adding to the world's misery.

Choosing a Life in the Dark Age

You make what seems a simple choice: choose a man or a job or a neighborhood—and what you have chosen is not a man or a job or a neighborhood, but a life.

~ Jessamyn West

IT SEEMS RIDICULOUS THAT even though abortions have been legal for over forty years, I kept my abortion secret for decades because I was ashamed. I learned this shame growing up in the dark age. In that dark age, my family and most of society did not talk about sex. Ever. Mentioning sex and anything connected to sexual activity was as taboo then as homosexuality and same-sex marriages were just a few years ago. References to sex-related topics were coded and made in hushed tones. We referred to a woman expecting a baby as being "infamilyway" or "knocked up." Female and male genitals were referred to as "privates," and women's monthly menses were called "periods," or more crudely, "being on the rag." The act of sexual intercourse was alluded to with words like "whatchamacallit," or by a certain facial expression. This avoidance and denial made sex mysterious and alluring, but it also stigmatized what is a natural and universal behavior.

When I was a young woman, contraception was unreliable and difficult to come by; "the pill"was nearly a decade away. Educating young people about their sexuality was not even a distant consideration. As I grew up, I learned about "doing it," the playground term for sexual intercourse, from girls slightly less ignorant than I was. I did know a baby took nine months to be born. I also knew, because of the sad looks and gossip, that females (of any age) who were infamilyway without being married, were objects of pity, ridicule or shame—most often all three. I couldn't understand why these women, whom my mother and

3

aunt whispered about, would continue "doing it" for nine straight months when they knew it was wrong to have a baby out-of-wedlock. Abortions were illegal, so women either gave birth engulfed in disapproval or broke the law. When I found myself in that position, I chose to commit a crime.

This was the way of life in the U.S. fifty years ago. However, some twenty-first century politicians seem determined to turn the clock back to those days when women were virtual prisoners of men's decisions about our reproductive rights. Back to when contraception was not easily available and abortions were a dangerous and illegal underground activity. I came of age during that backward era. It is not a time we should have to live through again.

I had been baffled about why male legislators have been so determined, not only to outlaw abortions again, but also to make it extremely difficult for women to obtain contraception. Why would they want to get women mad at them? I couldn't comprehend their reasoning at all. Then I read an article by **Sara Robinson** in which she described "the mass availability of nearly 100% effective contraception" as an "Innovation That Changed The World." Until birth control came along, she argued, "anatomy really was destiny — and all of the world's societies were organized around that central fact. Women were born to bear children; they had no other life options."

So, it really is about keeping women barefoot and pregnant! These insecure, patriarchal men who believe in things like "**legitimate rape**" and not funding Planned Parenthood are terrified of competing with women and cravenly disguise their fear as "religious liberty." Poor things, every time a woman advances to a sphere previously reserved for men, their balls must shrink.

Because I grew up in a hypercritical and repressive climate, I concealed my criminal act from everyone except my sister and sister-in-law. Even decades after the fact, I had shared my secret

4

with only two other close friends, because I still carried the guilt and mortification I felt at the time. I do not want us to return to that unreasonable judgmental period of our history, so I am sharing my story of what it was like in that dark age.

My mother, whose own mother had died when she was six years old, was a sly early feminist restricted by the norms of the day, but with firm convictions that she often repeated to my sister and me. When we began dating, Mama started "schooling" us about the opposite sex. When we married, she said, we should always let men *think* they were in charge; the implication being that we women were actually running things. She also shared her feelings about how unmarried girls having babies should be treated.

"You know when your Aunt Ollie was just sixteen she got infamilyway and old man Cheatham (Grandpa) put her out the house! I thought that was just awful, and Lillian (Grandma) let him do it! No man could ever make me put my daughter in the street at the time she needs somebody the most. Never!"

"What happened to Aunt Ollie?"

"I don't think Ollie ever got over that. And she was such a smart girl, too. Thank the Lord, the boy's mother took her in, but she wouldn't make that boy marry her."

At other times Mama would wag her head over the foolishness of parents who went too far in the opposite direction.

"Annette is infamilyway *again!*"

Annette was fifteen the first time she got pregnant and left town before she started showing. Shortly after she returned home, her parents adopted a baby that they were raising as their own. Everyone whispered that it was Annette's child, but publicly, it was her younger sister. Annette finished high school and seemed ready for a fresh start. Shortly after graduation, however, it was apparent she was expecting, but this time she didn't go away.

"That's what her folks get for making it too easy for her. If she had had to take care of that first child, I bet she would have thought twice before she got another one!" Then Mama would look my sister and me in the eye and say emphatically, "If a child of mine thinks she's grown enough to have a baby, she's grown enough to look after it! I'm not raising anybody else's children! All these fast girls do if you take the baby off their hands is go gallivanting off to get another one.

"Respectable women wait until they get married! These men will talk you into letting them use you, but if something happens, you can't find 'em."

I still remember an incident that happened when I was about ten. A woman who attended our Baptist church, who was divorced with a son about my age, had a baby by the choir director. In a ritual of asking forgiveness for her "sin," she had to stand in front of the congregation and be publicly shamed or "churched" during Sunday morning services. If a woman refused to participate in the shaming, she was barred from all church activities; excommunicated, if you will. Most startling to my young mind, was that, although everybody seemed to know who the father was, no mention was made of "churching" the married choir director. It was as if the baby had been created by immaculate conception.

Several girls I knew who were my age had "shotgun weddings" when they learned they were pregnant. A friend of mine who'd married just out of high school because she was expecting, quickly had three children. I rarely saw her anymore, but when I did, she looked utterly defeated. I knew from our occasional conversations that she and her husband were struggling mightily to hold things together. She had planned to attend college and become a teacher, but that path seemed closed or at best postponed indefinitely.

I was not going to be one of these women.

Although the actual word was never uttered, I had an abortion in 1957, sixteen years before Roe v. Wade, and about a decade before abortions were legal anywhere in the U.S. By the time Roe was passed in 1973, a few states had already legalized abortion. Women with the means to do so traveled to those states to have legal and safe abortions. In the mid-fifties that was not possible. My options were to have an out-of-wedlock baby or an illegal abortion.

I had completed my second year of college and first year on the Bloomington campus of Indiana University. Open displays of affection were commonplace on campus and sexual intercourse, "getting a piece," was a favorite discussion. I couldn't engage in these conversations because my sexual exploration had gone to the brink of actual intercourse, but never beyond. I was definitely aroused at the prospect of "going all the way," and becoming more willing to disregard my mother's dire warnings. One older student in our women's dorm persistently ridiculed me. "Girl, you don't know what you're missing!" I felt like a backward klutz. Every young man I went out with seemed eager to usher me into the inclusive getting-a-piece club so I was feeling pressure all around. One of those eager young men was a guy at home I'll call Fred.

On *that night*, for some reason I don't recall, everybody in my family was out of the house. It was late spring and I had an overwhelming desire to see Fred, so I called and invited him over. While I waited for him to arrive, I lost some of my bravado—what if my sister, brother or parents returned earlier than expected? We could not do it in the house. When Fred arrived, we drove to a secluded spot and climbed into the back of the car. Fred was startled at my unexpected cooperation, but not the least hesitant. We went at it, and woo-hoo! It was just as great as I'd been told! My sudden wild desire had been fueled by a year of sex talk, but was mostly driven by gamboling hormones. I later figured out I was ovulating! At the time I was all but totally ignorant of the mechanics of reproduction. I just wanted to know where and when Fred and I could do it again. I needn't have concerned myself, he made plans for that.

Two weeks later my menses didn't show. Really? Surely not! It couldn't be! Every day I checked. Not a pink drop. I was quaking with terror, certain that my mother knew I was late because she was vigilant about checking my and my sister's periods. I was also throwing up every morning, fortunately *after* I got to work, but I knew nothing of morning sickness, so I attributed it to anxiety. My whole being was heavy with dread when another month passed and still there was no sign of menstruation. I had missed *two whole months*! I fervently prayed for some other explanation. I knew women didn't get pregnant *every* time they did it, so perhaps something else had stopped my periods. Talking to my mother about it was out of the question.

I had to find out for sure what was happening, so I went to see our family doctor without telling anyone. Dr. B confirmed my worst fear. He knew I was not married and that I was in college. The tears rolling down my cheeks told him I was not ready to become a mother.

"I know a man, a physician, who can help you, if you don't want to have the baby. He's expensive, but he knows what he's doing, and I'll take care of you afterward."

I had heard whispers of women "getting rid of babies," and never thought I'd be one of them, but I didn't hesitate. "Yes, please tell me how to get in touch with him! Oh, thank you, Dr. B. Thank you!"

This physician he referred me to, whom I'll call Dr. Noble, had lost his license for performing abortions, but maintained a thriving business nonetheless. His fellow physicians obviously supported him, possibly receiving referral fees for sending clients. Dr. Noble charged $150.00 for his services at a time when routine visits to the doctor cost about ten dollars. So long as abortions were illegal, women didn't flinch at his price because it was far less than the cost of having an unwanted child.

I called Fred to tell him what was happening.

He interrupted angrily, "Why you telling me? I'm not getting married!"

"Nobody wants to get married; I'm not having the baby. I just need help paying for the doctor. It costs $150."

"I don't have any money!" His tone was harsh and accusatory as if I had deliberately betrayed him.

Fred's callous response was devastating. Although we were not in a serious relationship, I thought he cared enough about me to offer comfort, even if he couldn't help financially. What an idiot I was, having sex with an asshole who would treat me like that. I was humiliated, deeply ashamed and up to my eyeballs in guilt. Mama had warned us about this very thing and she was right. Now I was paying the price. Never again!

Dr. Noble performed his service in the client's home, but no way could he come to my parents' house. My sister-in-law had a son before she married my brother, and we were close, so I hoped she would understand. I told her what I was up to and she sympathized immediately. Without any questions or comments, she said Dr. Noble could perform the abortion at her apartment while she was at work. She lent me her house key and never spoke of it again. I was desperate and about to commit a crime; I didn't need additional grief, and she didn't bring me any. I was deeply grateful for that.

On the day of the procedure, I was terrified because I had no idea what was about to happen. What would Dr. Noble do to me? Would it hurt? But my fear didn't matter because it had to be done. Dr. Noble arrived on time, made his preparations, laid out his instruments, then asked me to lie down on the edge of the bed and remove my panties. He put a towel under my rear end and told me to spread my legs and hold them up.

I closed my eyes. I could feel the cold steel being inserted deep in my vagina, into my lower abdomen, then several uncomfortable pinches, but it didn't hurt. After working with the instruments, he packed my vagina with sterile gauze and told me to expect it to pass within the next twenty-four hours. He was there no more than half an hour, much less time than I had expected.

I had often stayed overnight with my sister-in-law to keep her company because my brother was away in the army, so my doing so did not alarm anyone. During the night I was awakened by pain so intense it made me nauseous. I spent most of the night in the bathroom with severe stomach cramps and vomiting. I could feel something pulling away from my body and pressing to come out. After several hours, and in an excruciating finale, I passed a lump. I looked into the toilet bowl and saw what looked like a large blood clot an inch or so in diameter floating in bloody water. I quickly flushed it away.

What a tremendous relief! My period was back. Hallelujah! But the ordeal wasn't over. I was sick and weak and bleeding profusely. Dr. Noble had advised me to have plenty of Kotex ready, so I was prepared. I spent two nights with my sister-in-law. On the third day, she took me home and I got in bed. I called Dr. B who gave me instructions and said he'd make a house call, which he later did.

I believe my mother suspected what was going on, because she never asked a single question, and that was definitely *not* her way. When I heard her on the telephone telling somebody I had the flu, I was certain she knew and was relieved I would not be shaming the family by having an "illegitimate" baby. She was probably pleased I had taken care of it without involving her. We never talked about it.

Within a few days, I was feeling better and able to go to Dr. B.'s office for a thorough examination. He did a D & C (**Dilation and Curettage**) to be certain I recovered without complications. Instead of returning to campus that fall, I took classes locally and continued working full-time to replenish the tuition funds I'd spent on the abortion.

I was fortunate that when I got pregnant long before I was ready to parent, I was a grown woman. I had seen the lives of teens who became parents before they were ready, and I didn't want that life. I doubt that Dr. B would have referred me to Dr.

Noble if I had not been an adult. Without access to a competent abortionist, I would have been forced to resort to the coat-hanger/knitting needle method that many women used to end their unwanted pregnancies. I knew about women rushed to the hospital because of botched attempts performed at low or no cost by "somebody somebody knew" or by relatives. Women had died, been maimed, or been rendered sterile from such efforts. Those who currently advocate curtailing access to birth control and abortion apparently have not considered that their efforts will only increase the number of unwanted children born to women who don't have the money to seek alternatives. Those with means will travel to places where contraception and abortions are available.

Had I given birth, I would have been a frustrated, uneducated young mom with a child who didn't know her/his father. Possibly I could have become a recipient of public assistance. Instead, I chose the life I wanted, completed college, had a career and became a parent when I was ready for that responsibility.

Secrets are debilitating. Hiding a part of yourself carves a hole in your heart in which you enclose the anguished knowledge. The more of yourself you keep hidden, the larger the hole grows until gloom reigns throughout your life. I'm revealing my secret not only to disperse the gloom and relieve myself of that burden, but also to inform those who don't know what it was like in that dark age when males dictated what happened with our bodies. It was a time of shame, anxiety and terror for women. We can't go back there again.

Links:

Sara Robinson http://www.alternet.org/story/154144/why_patriarchal_men_are_utterly_petrified_of_birth_control_--_and_why_we%27ll_still_be_fighting_about_it_100_years_from_now?akid=8270.34521.aRSTza&rd=1&t=8

legitimate rape http://www.newser.com/story/190747/todd-akin-not-sorry-for-rape-comments-after-all.html

Dilation and Curettage http://womenshealth.about.com/cs/surgery/a/d_and_c.htm

Expanding Possibilities

In every moment of our existence, we are in that field of all
possibilities where we have access to an infinity of choices.

~ **Deepak Chopra**

"MA, I'M GETTING MARRIED. Her name is Janet and she's a Negro."

Art and I had discussed this. I thought it would be better to
let them discover what I looked like when we met. But Art liked
people to know he was marrying a black woman; it corroborated
his standing as a political radical.

"A Negro!" He reported his mom said this with alarm. "A
schvartz? But they're not our people!"

"Well, Ma, you know the Yemenite Jews are black."

"Oh! Is she Jewish?" Art said his mother sounded somewhat
relieved at this possibility.

He admitted that I was not Jewish. I suppose the comment
about the Yemenis was meant to assure her that if there were
black Jews somewhere in the world, people of my hue were not
irredeemable. Of course, I doubt that people from Yemen consider themselves to be black.

After reporting on this conversation with his mother, Art
asked, "What about your parents? Will they have a problem with
me being a Jew?"

"No, not at all. My mother just wants me to be married. So far
as your religion goes, she'll be happy to know that you have one."

Despite my cavalier assessment, I hadn't told my family. How
could I tell them I was getting married, *again*. Not even two
years had passed since I shamed them by getting a divorce. More
than that, though, I was decidedly uncomfortable with the idea
myself. Not only was I about to get married, but I was marrying a
white man whom I barely knew. There was no way to justify it. I'd

tell them after the fact. If I had been euphorically in love, maybe I wouldn't have cared how they felt, but I wasn't. I'd married for love once and that didn't work; maybe this would. I grew up in Indianapolis, Indiana, possibly the most southern of northern cities. My parents had migrated from the rural South hoping for a better shot at life in the urban North than they could expect in their birthplaces. I was nurtured and loved in our close-knit family, where books and reading were valued so I had no real need to escape. I read everything I could get my hands on and what I read made me long for something more! I had no idea *what*, but I felt there had to be more to life than what I was experiencing. When I graduated college, I chose to leave home and seek those elusive *possibilities*.

It was 1965 and the civil rights movement was gathering steam, but interracial marriages were still hard to find, especially between a black woman and a white man. In fact, the 1960 census reported that 99.6 percent of marriages were between people of the same color. Black men married white women in the places where interracial marriages were allowed, but white men had a long tradition of raping and using black women that had begun during slavery. White men, with impunity, could beat or kill any black man who objected to the exploitation or abuse of his wife, mother or sister. During the hundreds of years of African enslavement, the custom was that white men (particularly those of the wealthier classes) used black women to satisfy their sexual desires because their wives were "too refined" for the crudeness of sex. The wide spectrum of skin colors among blacks is testament to this long-standing tradition.

Even after slavery was abolished, black women working as domestic servants were preyed upon by their white male employers. A high-profile example of this practice was made public in 2003 when **Essie Mae Washington-Williams** revealed that she was the daughter of the late segregationist U.S. senator Strom Thurmond. Her teenage mother was a servant in the Thurmond household when Strom impregnated her. The bottom line was that no "respectable" white man ever *married* the black woman with whom he had sex. In fact, nearly every state in the U.S. at one time or another considered such marriages as verboten as same-sex marriages were in 2008. Interracial unions did not become legal throughout the country until 1967 with the U.S. Supreme Court decision in Loving *v.* Virginia. When Art and I married in 1965, laws in sixteen states made marriages between blacks and whites a criminal offense. We were living in Michigan, whose ban had been repealed in 1883, so we could be legally married there.

A part of me wanted to defy these traditions and restrictions. I knew our marriage would be a novelty and that we might travel to places where we were breaking the law. True, I wasn't giddily in love, but I certainly enjoyed Art and welcomed the idea of new experiences. With him I'd get an up-close and personal look at academia, Jews, and white people. I knew little about those worlds and was curious to learn more.

I had met Art three months earlier at a CORE party in Ann Arbor. I was in Ann Arbor taking a Saturday morning class at the University of Michigan (U of M). I enrolled in the class mostly as an excuse to get out of Saginaw on the weekends. It was my second year as a librarian at Saginaw's Mac Arthur High School. My first year had been a social desert, so I had to do something, and Ann Arbor was less than a two-hour drive away. I didn't know anybody there, but a friend put me in touch with her friend, Gloria, who invited me to stay with her. The first time we met, Gloria asked if I'd like to attend a CORE party with her the next Saturday night. *Would I? Absolutely!* Gloria was white, but I knew there would be plenty of black folk at a CORE party. That meant I could easily meet some fine activist brother. I *knew* Ann Arbor would be an improvement over Saginaw.

CORE (the Congress of Racial Equality) was riding high in 1965. The civil rights group had been founded in 1942 by James Farmer, the first president, and both black and white students on the campus of the University of Chicago. They organized to desegregate public accommodations in Chicago, and after that success they went national. Their fame spread when they tested the legality of segregation on interstate bus travel in the South with their **Freedom Rides** in 1961. CORE's members were largely black and white college students.

In those days, we dressed to look our best for parties—blue jeans had not become de rigueur for every occasion. When I packed for that second weekend in Ann Arbor, I included an outfit that always got lots of compliments: a chocolate-brown double-knit jacket and skirt that I wore with a brightly-colored print blouse. When the brothers scanned the party and saw me, I wanted them to feel like monarch butterflies spotting a zinnia.

The party was held in the home of a young professor and his wife. The frame house was an elegant high-ceilinged Victorian-era two-story with a parlor separated from the sitting room by open French doors. The sitting room opened into the dining room, behind which was a kitchen. When Gloria and I arrived every room was filled with people. *Yes!* Many of them were white, but just as I'd hoped, there were lots of brothers. Gloria introduced me as we moved through the crowd. Whenever I met a brother, I offered a welcoming, modestly flirtatious smile, but none of them so much as made eye contact. A couple of them looked longingly at Gloria, but all I got was a terse acknowledgment of the introduction. Not one of the brothers expressed the slightest curiosity about me. What was going on? Never had I been at a party in which I was completely ignored by *every man in the room.*

After about an hour of this, I literally stepped aside to check out the gathering. I was not accustomed to whites and blacks partying together. I had attended Indiana University, and on that campus there was occasional sly interracial dating, but I'd never heard of an interracial party. I had already noticed that the crowd was largely white, but in looking more closely, I saw that among the hundred or more revelers there were a number of black men, but only one other black woman. And every brother there was either huddled with a white woman or eyeing one. I was definitely *not* on their agenda that evening. Interracial dating, furtive for so long, had erupted in the civil rights movement like Mt. Sinabung, the Sumatran volcano that had been dormant for four hundred years. And the brothers were taking full advantage.

Well, two can play that game—I'll talk to the white guys.

I'd dated a couple of white men before, so this would not be unfamiliar territory. I looked around the party for an appealing-looking white guy and quickly found one. He was standing alone in front of the fireplace, tall with dark hair and a beard. (I was smitten with beards.) I walked over to chat him up, but soon learned that he and his wife were the party hosts. *So much for him.* Continuing my sortie, I wandered into the dining room and saw another dark-haired bearded guy. He was standing in the doorway to the kitchen talking to a couple of people. My new target was good-looking, but short, not much taller than me. I noticed that he was wearing the Urban League's familiar symbol, a white button bearing a black equal sign, in the lapel of his jacket. After I pushed past him to go into the kitchen, I pointed to the button and facetiously asked, "What does that mean?"

He turned to me and said, "It means, 'Equal rights for all.'"

"And does 'all' include people like me?"

"Of course. 'All' means everybody."

I looked him in the eye and said, "I've seen very little evidence of that."

He grinned, held out his hand, and said, "Hi. I'm Art Saxe. What's your name?"

Art was also visiting Ann Arbor for the weekend; he'd lived

there while doing graduate work in anthropology at U of M. We talked for a while, then he disappeared. I didn't see him again until the party was winding down and those who remained were gathering to watch him perform. Accompanying himself first on guitar, then on banjo, Art sang traditional folk songs from various cultures including some blues numbers. His voice wasn't great, but he was an impressive and charming entertainer. I was astonished that this young white guy knew my people's music. I hadn't thought whites were interested in black music except to make money from it. When Art finished his set he walked over to me.

"Can I take you home?"

We rode to Gloria's in his cream-colored Volvo and talked some more. He was from Brooklyn and was a dissertation away from completing his Ph.D. A few months earlier he had moved to Mt. Pleasant, a small college town west of Saginaw, to teach at Central Michigan University (CMU). Art asked if he could see me again, so we exchanged phone numbers.

Ah, I thought, this could be interesting: a single professor from New York City, *and* active in the civil rights movement! But I didn't really expect to hear from him again, and I was certainly not going to call him!

Art did call and he invited me to Mt. Pleasant for an event the following Saturday, which meant I wouldn't be spending the weekend in Ann Arbor. He asked me to drive over, but I didn't want him to think I was *that* eager to see him. I told him he'd have to pick me up in Saginaw. Art drove the fifty-plus miles to Saginaw and picked me up. We went back to Mt. Pleasant for the event, then he drove me back home. I insisted he come pick me up whenever we saw each other.

Not only did Art play black music, but he had an impressive collection of blues albums at his apartment. Lightnin' Hopkins, Sonny Terry, Huddie "Leadbelly" Ledbetter and Brownie Mc-Ghee were among the blues artists in his collection. His library included books like *The Souls of Black Folk* by W.E.B. Du Bois and James Baldwin's *Nobody Knows My Name*. And he had read them. I didn't know many people of *any* color with whom I could discuss such books.

After a couple of months Art grew weary of driving to Saginaw every weekend and came up with an idea, "Why don't we move in together and get a place halfway between here and Mt. Pleasant, like Midland?"

"Are you kidding? Living in Saginaw is bad enough; I certainly don't want to live in some other tiny little town." I figured there wouldn't be any black folk in Midland. "Besides, I'm not going to *live* with you!" *Those days are over, buddy!*

"But I'm not ready to get married."

"Who said anything about getting married? If you're tired of driving over here every weekend, come every *other* weekend." I was aghast that he thought I would *shack up* with him! My family and friends would be horrified if I allowed a *white* man to use me like that.

Art was not happy with my solution; he wanted us to spend more time together, not less; a short time later, he asked me to marry him. *He must be crazy; we just met.* But what I said was, "Let me think about it."

The next time I saw Art, he was excited, "Janet, we need to go shopping for wedding clothes."

"Wedding clothes! What are you talking about? We're not getting married; I haven't made up my mind yet."

"Seriously? I thought you were just being coy." Art was genuinely surprised.

"Coy!? We barely know each other."

"We know we want to be together, and you won't move in with me, so we have to get married. I've already applied for the license and made an appointment for us to get blood tests. And a guy in my department is planning a reception for us at his place afterward."

Woohooo! This man reeeeally wants to marry me!

I was flattered a white professor wanted to marry me, would not, in fact, take no for an answer. Not that I ever said, "No." I was hesitant, but the prospect of an entirely new kind of life was irresistible. We went shopping. Then one day Art showed up with the marriage license. I had no idea he could get a license without my signature, but I was wrong, obviously. When he started talking about the reception in Mt. Pleasant, it dawned on me that I might be the only black person there. I hurriedly invited my cousin Odahlia and her family, and Marian, the one black friend I'd made in Saginaw.

Art and I were married December 18, 1965; he was thirty and I was twenty-eight, both Taureans with May birthdays. The short ceremony took place at the rural home of a justice of the peace whose yard was thick with mud. Boards had to be laid between the car and front porch so we could go inside without messing up our new clothes and shoes. After the ceremony we went directly to the reception, which was held at the home of one of Art's colleagues.

As a wedding gift, Art's friends Lew and Sally Binford sent us airline tickets to Santa Barbara, California. It would be my second flight and first trip to California. We used the tickets for a honeymoon trip during our winter break. Before we left, I told my family I'd gotten married and gave them my new address.

"I can't believe you would be so foolish!" Mama's fury caught me completely off-guard. She was not concerned that I had married again so soon, but rather that I had married a *Jew!* I had no idea she despised Jews. The only mention of Jews in our house had been biblical references. On the other hand, I'm sure it didn't occur to her that she'd ever have one in the family. From then on, Mama's calls and letters honed in on the perils of being married to a Jew. She actually said, "Be careful, Jews will work you to death."

"Ma, I don't work for Art; he's my husband."

My mother's social life—church, civic activities, friends, relatives—was entirely black; her contact with Jews, or any whites, was essentially in cleaning and doing laundry for them. Her opinion was shaped by a lifetime of encounters with racial discrimination and her well-founded perception that whites regarded her primarily as a workhorse. My experience was different, largely because I'd had contacts with whites as peers—in high school and college and at work. However, like her, I'd learned that whites were all-powerful and that our goal as blacks was to be as much like them as possible. Jews were white. Shouldn't she be happy I had taken a step up and married into the privileged race? Other blacks, usually men, were also offended by my marriage. Some accused me of joining the enemy, and others asked how I could allow a *white* man to touch me after the hell they'd put us through. On the other hand some blacks, women in particular, applauded me for "landing" not only a white professor, but a *Jew!* Everybody knew Jews have money.

Meanwhile, Art had the last laugh. After we married, we lived in Mt. Pleasant, so *I* was the one driving to Saginaw—*every day*—to go to work. My apartment was definitely the better space, but I had a roommate, so we moved into Art's place on the first floor of an old frame house. The landlady, Ruby, lived on the upper floor, and we used the same washer and dryer. Each of us had access to the laundry room through different doors that could be locked behind us when we finished. When Ruby saw me doing laundry she assumed Art had hired a maid, and a black woman *working* in her house was not a problem. Soon Ruby learned that I was Art's wife, *living* in her house. She hit the ceiling and told Art we had to move immediately. Then she locked the door to the laundry room.

Art was outraged. "She can't do this! I'm calling the police! She can't force me to move because I married a Negro!"

"Where have you been? The police won't do anything. People are always telling us where we can and cannot live. This might be the first time it happened *after* a Negro moved in, but it happens all the time."

"She is *not* getting away with this!"

"I don't care what happens to her." Ruby wasn't the first racist I'd encountered, but I didn't want to live under the same roof with one. Who knew what she might do; after all, she had access to all of our things. I wanted out of there, probably more than she wanted us gone. Art, on the other hand, was not about to be pushed around. He raised hell at CMU until an official warned Ruby that she would be removed from their list of approved housing if she didn't back off. The threat to her pocketbook worked like magic, and we immediately regained access to the laundry room.

One scrumptious surprise in my new marriage was that for the first time in my life I did not have to pinch pennies. Our combined annual earnings were over $12,000 at a time when the median family income in the U.S. was $6,900. Never before had I been able to buy and do whatever I wanted without agonizing over prices. When I shopped for groceries, I bought expensive steaks like the ones I had served the Teetors when I worked as a maid. We entertained often, and our liquor cabinet was well stocked. Sometimes when friends came over Art would make a couple of large thin-crust pizzas with lots of toppings. He was proud of his ability to make pizzas from scratch, including tossing and spinning the dough, and he owned all the equipment—a rolling pin, large flat pans and a circular pizza knife.

Still, I did not enjoy Mt. Pleasant; it was smaller and duller than Saginaw. I especially loathed living in Ruby's dumpy old house with its outdated wiring. Not to mention I was sick of driving to Saginaw every day. I leaned on Art to move to Ann Arbor. I told him he could finish his Ph.D. and get a professorship in some livelier place, maybe even in another country. Either I was persuasive, or Art was also ready to leave. That June

I resigned as Mac Arthur's head librarian, and Art left CMU.

In Ann Arbor we sublet an apartment for the summer and looked for permanent housing. We found a well-kept two-story frame house on Spring Street and signed a year's lease. It had a living room, dining room, and large kitchen on the first floor, and two bedrooms and a bathroom upstairs. Neither Art nor I had ever had that much living space and we loved it! We furnished the place with the things from each of our apartments. And because we had room, our house became a gathering place for friends, meetings, and parties. When Floyd McKissick, who succeeded James Farmer as national director of CORE, came to town, we were honored to have him spend the night in our spare bedroom.

That time in Ann Arbor remains a cherished memory. Aside from my college days I had rarely been around intellectuals— people who read deeply and were educated beyond high school. Most folk I knew talked about other people or their material possessions, not books and ideas. In our Ann Arbor circle nearly everyone had a degree and several were engaged in advanced graduate study. For the first time I was hanging out with a range of accomplished people, including physicists, archeologists, physicians, community organizers, and artists. I eagerly listened and offered my own opinions on all manner of topics—escalation of the war in Vietnam, the civil rights movement, religion, cultural mores, and politics, including **Edward Brooke**'s election to the U.S. Senate. (Brooke, from Massachusetts, was the first black senator since Reconstruction.)

Much of the conversation in our house centered on anthropology and I was intrigued by the talk about the ethnic groups Art and his colleagues were studying in different parts of the world. I'm not sure I'd ever heard the word "anthropology" before, but I was fascinated by the similarities among different peoples in various places, no matter how simple or complex their social organizations. I decided to take some anthropology courses. My classes and discussions with Art helped me see racial strife in the U.S. from a broader perspective. I learned that the conditions of blacks in this country are similar to those of oppressed people elsewhere. Blacks are not the only aggrieved people, and skin color not the only reason people are subjugated. It became clear to me that human behavior is identical around the world; groups just have different social practices and rationales for their mores. The more I learn, the more that understanding has been reinforced.

I was also noticing that Art had an unfamiliar kind of confidence. I had to adjust to his expectation that he would be respected no matter where we went. We were often the object of stares and double takes, but nobody *ever* said anything to us. I was not comfortable with what I felt was unfriendly attention, but Art delighted in our presence surprising people. We casually entered elegant restaurants, hotels, and shops where, alone, I would have been skeptical about my reception. Some maitre d's and salesclerks were obviously startled, but never rude. Late one night we were driving on a back road somewhere in Michigan and Art needed to use the restroom. He stopped at the first open gas station, and I nearly cautioned him about getting out of the car in that isolated place, but then I remembered, "He's white; nothing will happen."

I had been admitted to U of M for my prior course work as "not a candidate for a degree." I was taking those classes primarily to expand my social life. Not only that, but I was too relieved and emotionally drained after getting my bachelor's degree to be interested in submitting to the grind again. However, I did enjoy taking classes for the fun of learning.

Art said it didn't make sense to take classes without being formally admitted and he insisted that I apply to U of M's Horace H. Rackham School of Graduate Studies. Although I'd received two A's in the U of M courses I'd taken previously, my average as an undergraduate was barely a C. I didn't expect a prestigious grad school like Rackham to admit me and wasn't surprised when there was no response to my application. But I wanted a decision before I enrolled and decided to call, fully expecting to be denied. Art wouldn't hear of my calling. He knew about my undergraduate grades and was insistent that I go visit the graduate office, saying, "They won't turn you down to your face."

I figured they *would* indeed turn me down to my face, but decided to try Art's suggestion anyway. At the graduate office I told the receptionist why I was there. She went to a file cabinet and found my folder, which included a half-page form. She read the form, then placed a check mark in the box beside "admitted," and handed me a carbon copy of it. I was stunned. A clerk had just admitted me to the University of Michigan graduate school. I've never forgotten that. It was easy. I had merely inquired and it was done! I felt like I had just learned a white people secret. Without Art's urging I would never have made a personal visit to that office. It's not that I'm reticent, but I had been carefully trained not to assert myself—it wasn't ladylike, and more important, drawing the attention of whites might only remind them of how much they loathed you. It was best to remain quietly amiable around the people who could, on an impulse, make your life extremely difficult.

That experience taught me not to accept rejection *before* encountering it.

Links:

Essie Mae Washington-Williams http://www.nytimes.com/2005/02/06/opinion/6sun3.html?_r=0

Freedom Rides http://www.pbs.org/wgbh/americanexperience/freedomriders/

Edward Brooke http://www.britannica.com/EBchecked/topic/81200/Edward-Brooke

✼

For Love of a Child:
My Journey to Health

*Until you've [had a child] you're just guessing about love,
gesturing toward it, assuming that it's the right name for a
feeling you've had.*

~ Caitlin Flanagan

"**JANET, YOU'VE GOT CANCER** and need surgery right away."

I answered the telephone to hear my gynecologist, without
fanfare or preamble, say those alarming words. Terror choked off
my breathing for a few seconds. Fear gripped my body as if a gi-
ant clamp were squeezing me. Cancer? Not on top of everything
else! How could this be happening to *me*? My stomach churned
while I fought the idea I had "the big C." In the early 1970s, the
word itself was rarely mentioned openly. People kept their diagnosis secret, because to talk about having cancer was the same as
saying, "I'm about to die;" and we denied even the possibility of
death until it actually happened.

My father had died a month earlier and I was still in Indianapolis when I got this news. I knew Daddy was critically ill but
figured he'd recover because he was only seventy years old! We
expected him to live to be nearly ninety, like Grandpa had. But
just like that, he was gone. I would never again witness his joy
in life, and he wouldn't be there to turn to for help and advice.
He and Mama were the pillars holding my life erect and one had
vanished. I was unbalanced, exposed, weakened. We didn't know
he died of cancer until we read the death certificate.

When my older brother called a couple of months earlier
to tell me that our dad was gravely ill, I immediately gathered
up Kamau, my eight-month-old baby, and went home. Daddy's
illness gave me a reason to get away from Kamau's dad. I had

thought he was the love of my life—that, to paraphrase John Donne, "Our two souls were one." The passion was so intense, though, it was frightening. We were unsure of ourselves in this unfamiliar landscape, and consequently, unsure of each other. What we were sure of was exactly where to inflict a wound on the other that would cause the most pain. He left on an "errand" on New Year's Eve when I was eight months pregnant and extremely vulnerable, and did not return until the next day. I was home alone *all night*. I felt abandoned, unloved, and deeply hurt. After Kamau's birth, he periodically lacerated me by leaving evidence of his infidelity where I could not miss it. Perhaps he was terrified of his new responsibility. He had told me he wasn't ready to be a father but my clock was ticking so I flippantly responded, "Well you'd better stop doing what you've been doing then."

I was angry and confused, emotionally wrung out from caring for a new baby and being tortured by the man I loved. I was completely dependent because I hadn't worked since a few weeks before Kamau's birth. Adding to my despair was the terror of knowing we would not be rearing our child together. There was no way I could accept this rack of humiliation he'd apparently designed for me. I needed to find a nanny and get back to work so I could move on. I had interviewed a couple of potential nannies, but the only person I really trusted to care for my son was my mother. But Mama was in Indiana and I was in California.

By the time the commotion of Daddy's funeral was over in late September, I'd decided that the best thing for me, and Mama, was for me to move back home. I could help my mother—who was the original unliberated woman and had never lived alone—and she could look after Kamau while I went back to work. We would recover together. I took a quick trip back to California to arrange for the move and returned to Indianapolis, where I began a frustrating search for a job.

It was disheartening that everywhere I went I was asked to take a typing test. As my resume clearly stated, I had just left the English doctoral program at Stanford University. I was exasperated and disgusted that employers in my hometown were still not willing to consider blacks for professional positions. While I was job hunting I made an appointment with a gynecologist to check on a vicious vaginal discharge. It was a few days after that examination that my doctor unceremoniously broke the news of my diagnosis.

So there I was, unemployed and separated from my baby's father. I always turned to Daddy in such crises, but he was gone. And now I had cancer with no health insurance! *What else could go wrong?!* I felt as if I had been plunged under water and all sights and sounds were being distorted as they tried to reach me.

I remained lucid that calamitous year only by loving and caring for Kamau.

The doctor said I had stage IV cervical cancer, which meant that it had likely spread to infect adjacent tissues and organs. My first thought on hearing that was, "I'm going to die." In a flash, I had another thought, "I *can't* die and leave Kamau." I went for a second opinion, hoping my gynecologist had made a mistake. The second doctor confirmed the diagnosis, adding his own urgent warning that I needed surgery immediately.

OKAY, SO I HAVE CANCER. But instead of despair, I felt defiant. Fortunately, I'd heard stories about a couple of people who had survived cancer. One was a distant cousin who lived into her eighties some twenty years after being told she had breast cancer. So, I knew it was *possible* to live after being diagnosed with the dreaded disease.

First, I *had* to find a job. If I was employed, I'd have health insurance to pay for the surgery. Still there were no employers willing to hire me in anything other than clerical positions, which my pride did not allow me to consider. Thanksgiving came and went with no employment prospects. Mama, fearing another death from cancer, urged me to have the surgery first, then look for a job. I wasn't getting anywhere on the job front, so I agreed. Who knew what might happen if I continued to postpone surgery? Since Christmas was going to be sad enough without Daddy, I didn't want to make it grimmer by being in the hospital. I asked the doctor to schedule surgery as soon as possible after the holidays. I knew I could not be admitted to the hospital where he was on staff without proof of insurance, so I went to Blue Cross-Blue Shield and made an initial payment on an individual health insurance policy. I was sure my pre-existing condition would not be covered, but at least the insurance card would get me into the hospital. I'd figure out how to pay later.

One day after everything was all set for the surgery, I was walking down Washington Street. I don't remember where I was going, but I'll never forget the experience. With conviction and total resolve I said to myself, "I.AM.NOT.GOING.TO.DIE." At that moment the fear that had unconsciously been lodged in my gut since the doctor's initial pronouncement of cancer, drained away. I felt a rush of strength and renewal in my body and absolutely *knew* I would be fine. Later I read the spiritual teacher Deepak Chopra's explanation that being in *dharma* means "you are on the correct path spiritually." At that moment I believe I assimilated my *dharma*. And that was just the tip of the *dharma* iceberg.

Many years later, I learned that cancer cells are actually weak and confused, and that we all occasionally produce abnormal, cancerous cells, but our healthy immune systems routinely destroy them. According to Dr. Carl Simonton of the Simonton Cancer Center, cancer is a *systemic* disorder that has the ability to spread, and that involves the entire organism—the mind as well as the body. He says that when the immune system is compromised by things like emotional stress the cancerous cells run amok. The stress suppresses the body's immune system and, at the same time, leads to hormonal imbalances that result in increased production of abnormal cells.

Systemic conditions for production of abnormal cells in my body were optimum when I was diagnosed. My hormones were out of whack from having just given birth; my emotions were battered by my mercurial relationship, and then my dad died.

I had surgery on January 4. Afterward the doctor told me the cancer was *in situ*, that is, localized, and he was able to remove it all. I did not require any further treatment. I have no doubt that my determination to be there for Kamau, the true love of my life, combined with my *dharma*, produced the miracle of a stage IV cancer shrinking to a localized one. A week after surgery I was home caring for my baby. Although he looked like any other year-old toddler, he was so heavy I called him "the lead-bottom boy." Mama had to take him out of his crib for several weeks before I was strong enough to pick him up. Years later, in Bernie Siegel's 1986 book *Love, Medicine and Miracles*, I read, "Unconditional love is the most powerful stimulant of the immune system. The truth is: love heals. Miracles happen to exceptional patients every day—patients who have the courage to love."

As soon as the doctor released me, I hit the streets, more determined than ever to find a job to my liking. Early in my renewed search, I ran into Art Rhea, a politically connected friend I had known for many years. I complained to him about being unable to find a professional position. Art said he knew somebody who could help, so I gave him a copy of my resume. He called the next day to tell me he'd set up a meeting with W. T. Ray, a member of his party who was executive assistant to Governor Otis R. Bowen. *Dharma* again: Mr. Ray and my dad had worked together as volunteers at the YMCA. He was pleased to spend a little clout on my behalf in homage to his recently deceased co-worker. (Daddy came through in a crisis again!) After reviewing my resume, Mr. Ray thought my education and experience could best be used in the Indiana Department of Public Instruction. He sent me to an associate superintendent *with his recommendation.* In that political environment, a recommendation from the governor's office was more like a command.

In March I began work as a curriculum consultant in the state's department of education. It was, by far, the best job I've ever had: it paid well, provided Blue Cross-Blue Shield health insurance, I wrote my own job description, and I largely operated autonomously. The hospital had just begun to bill me and I was now in position to make payments. After about three months, with a hefty portion of the hospital bill yet to be paid, *dharma* intervened. The hospital sent a statement saying that the remaining charges were covered by my insurance.

I learned something else from Siegel's *Love, Medicine and Miracles* that I now believe may have significantly impacted my immune system. I read that women who had lost a child were more susceptible to cancers of the reproductive system—uterus, cervix, ovaries. That statement hit me like a two-by-four in the face. I read it over and over. Unbelievable! How did Siegel know about my situation?

During my first marriage, twelve years before Kamau's birth, I had another son, Paul, who was born prematurely and died within three months. At the time of Paul's death, I shed few tears, refused to feel the pain and did everything possible to pretend I had not been shaken to the core by that loss. A couple of years later I fled the marriage, leaving my agony behind, or so I thought. (Wherever I go, there I am.) Instead, although I was oblivious to it, that deeply buried emotional wound was resuscitated by the second pregnancy. (Whatever you bury, is buried alive!) Although Kamau was obviously more robust than Paul, I checked him constantly to make sure he was still breathing. I didn't relax that routine until Kamau started walking at ten months. I was aware as I checked on him that I was driven by the fear he might die.

Siegel's observation meant that my cancer was possibly predictable! I've never had another cancer diagnosis, yet I sacrificed my remaining reproductive organs—uterus and ovaries—to that unacknowledged pain. I recently read a statement by psychoanalyst Alice Miller that resonated with me. She said, "The body will not stop tormenting us until we stop evading the truth." That was certainly my experience. Even after I read *Love, Medicine and Miracles,* it took psychotherapy, years of self-examination, spiritual searching and finally, writing a memoir*, before I was able to confront and explore the ache residing in my body. Even though forty-three years had passed, writing the chapters about my pregnancy, the premature birth, Paul's hospitalization and his death was an excruciating exercise. My writing group had so many questions about lapses in my narrative—the issues I didn't want to face—that I had to revise those passages over and over and over. When I finally had an acceptable version, I read it aloud to myself. Tears broke through at last. For three days, nearly nonstop, I moaned and sobbed full-bodied, rattling lamentations. When the crying ended, I felt cleansed, and also whole; as if the scattered pieces of my soul had been reunited after a long absence from each other. I told a friend, "I don't believe I'll ever be sick again." So far, except for succumbing to colds when I'm anxious or exhausted, I haven't been.

The Time and Place That Gave Me Life, Indiana University Press, 2007

Remembering Daddy
Smith Henry Cheatham

It doesn't matter who my father was; it matters who I
remember he was.

~ Anne Sexton

WHEN I LEFT INDIANA IN 1964, I felt like Frederick Douglass
did in 1838 when he escaped slavery. At the time Douglass said,
"For the moment the dreams of my youth and the hopes of my
[adult]hood were completely fulfilled. The bonds that had held
me…were broken. …A new world had opened upon me."

My bonds, of course, were emotional rather than physical,
but the feelings of freedom and possibility were the same. Now I
could discover myself, and be whoever I wanted to be. The people I met would have no preconceived expectations about how
the daughter of/the sister of/a southsider should behave. I would
not have to hear my mother's opinion of every decision I made
and feel the guilt of having disappointed her yet again. Most of
all, in a new place, I could relax knowing there was nobody to
report my whereabouts to Daddy. I swear, everybody in Indianapolis either knew him, or knew about him, so I was always
wary that something I might do would embarrass or make him
ashamed of me.

My first home on my own was in Saginaw, Michigan, where
I learned there were places with even thinner views of the world
than Indianapolis. Several months after I'd moved away, my siblings and I were called home because Daddy was ill.

Stumpf Brothers Meat Packers, where Daddy had worked for
more than forty years, were preparing to close and had laid off
their workers. The small family business had no retirement plan.

For the first time in four decades, Daddy was without an income. He'd never made much money, working two and sometimes three jobs to take care of four growing children. When Stumpf's laid him off, he was sixty-two years old and he panicked. How would he get another job at his age? He didn't consider retiring early on his social security because he was just a few years away from paying off the mortgage on the new house he'd had built in 1959. In his desperation Daddy took the first job he could find—working as a janitor in a high school. It was too strenuous for a man who hadn't lifted anything heavier than a grandbaby for many years. He collapsed at work.

"Daddy, go ahead and retire. We'll take care of the house note." The four of us had a quick meeting and decided that each of us could easily chip in twenty-five dollars a month to make the ninety-three dollar payment. We told Daddy what we decided.

"Aw naw!" Daddy was emphatic. "Parents take care of their children. Not the other way 'round."

"But Daddy, you've worked hard all your life and taken good care of us. It's not a problem for us. We want to do it." I tried to convince Daddy that it would be our pleasure to pay his note.

He wouldn't have it. "I can take care of myself."

Smith Henry Cheatham migrated from Tennessee to Indianapolis in 1922, seeking a better life in the city. His family labored as sharecroppers all of his life and were no better off than when they started. By the time he was nineteen, Daddy was tired of working that hard without getting anywhere. He was the oldest son and, as was the practice, went to work in the tobacco fields beside his parents as soon as he was big enough, about nine years old. His education ended with fourth grade.

Daddy arrived in a city that was as rigidly segregated as any-place in Tennessee and that soon became the national headquarters of a resuscitated Ku Klux Klan. Smith Cheatham took it in stride—racial oppression was an integral part of Negro life—and he got on about the business of living. He found work, married, had four children. When each day's labors were finished he spent countless hours helping to improve circumstances in his community. He loved people and would chat up anybody, black or white, which was unusual in a segregated city in pre–civil-rights-movement America. In 1939 when he decided to buy a house for his growing family, he found a place he could afford not far from Stumpf's in a "white" neighborhood. Somehow he convinced the real estate agent to sell it to him.

At six feet he was the tallest in his family, towering over both parents and his nine siblings. His muscles would be the envy of today's most buff athletes, but Daddy never spent a minute in a gym; he earned his muscles the old-fashioned way, by working hard and long at jobs that these days are assigned to machines. Although he may have been briefly between jobs, Daddy was never unemployed, not even during the Great Depression. He would do anything to earn a living so long as it was "honest work." He got his first job in Indianapolis after he had repeatedly been refused employment on a construction site. Daddy knew that if they saw how hard and efficiently he worked, he'd be hired, so he picked up an unused wheelbarrow, filled it with sand and delivered it to where the concrete was being mixed. He did this a few times and was hired that day.

My older brother got into serious trouble when he was fourteen. He was taunted by a group of white boys in our neighborhood. Because he was outnumbered, he pulled out his knife and swung it, cutting the boy closest to him just below his heart. In 1946, this kind of thing could get a black man locked up for life, if not lynched. For several nights gangs of whites drove past our house blowing their horns and yelling threats, but it never went beyond that; possibly because they suspected we might fight back. Daddy hired a friend of his who was one of Indianapolis's best lawyers. In arguing his case before the judge, the lawyer compared the background and families of my brother and the

34

boy he'd cut. With the city's influential blacks speaking and writing letters on our family's behalf, it was no contest. My brother spent the night he was arrested in jail, paid the injured boy's medical expenses and that was that. None of the white boys in the neighborhood ever picked a fight with him again.

Integrity and reliability were important to Daddy. He often said, "A man's word is his bond." Because he was so trustworthy, he was the dues-collecting financial secretary of his Masonic lodge for twenty-five years. They wouldn't have anybody else doing it until Daddy personally recommended and trained a young man to replace him. Black folk in the area came to Daddy for help with their problems. Because Daddy knew so many well-connected people, he was often able to offer assistance, or send them to someone who could provide what they needed. When he became a Notary Public his local status as "mayor of the south side" seemed official.

Daddy started a thriving chitlin' business when he discovered that his employer was discarding the hog guts. Whenever Daddy bought a car, he'd negotiate the best possible cash deal with the auto salesman, then get a no-interest loan from Stumpf's to consummate it. Using his charm and persuasive powers, he was regularly a top fund-raiser for the Senate Avenue (Colored) YMCA, despite his limited education. Except for my son, Kamau, who was born eight months before Daddy died and clearly inherited his spirit, as well as several of his physical characteristics, I've never known a more resourceful person than Smith Cheatham.

After Daddy's collapse at his new job, there was nothing we could say to convince him to take our money, so I decided to approach the problem from another angle.

A few months earlier Daddy had been honored with a testimonial dinner at the Fall Creek YMCA for his "outstanding contributions to the progress of Indianapolis." While working as a butcher and at any other manual labor he could find to support his family, Daddy had fed his intellect and desire for meaning with a commitment to volunteer work. Among the many roles he took on to help improve his community were founder and president of the Southeast Civic League, board member of the Senate Avenue (and later Fall Creek) YMCA, and chairman of the deacon board and superintendent of the Sunday school at our church. While my brothers were growing up, he took them and other neighborhood boys to the Y every Saturday.

It seemed to me that a man who had given so much might be due some consideration with his present dilemma, so I made an appointment to see Frank Lloyd. Dr. Lloyd was a physician and president of Methodist Hospital, the state's largest healthcare facility. He was what you might call Indianapolis's "Negro-in-Chief," the best-connected black man in the city. I told him about Daddy's many years of volunteer work and his current situation. Since Daddy insisted on working, I asked Dr. Lloyd if he could find something less strenuous for him to do. Dr. Lloyd didn't know Daddy personally, but he knew who he was, and he knew some of the people Daddy had worked with in the Y. Dr. Lloyd assured me he'd do whatever he could.

A couple of weeks after I returned to Saginaw, I got a call from Mama. She said that Bob DeFrantz, the director of Community Action Against Poverty (CAAP), had offered Daddy a job as a youth counselor. The DeFrantz family had known Daddy for many years. Bob's dad, Faburn E. DeFrantz Sr., was executive secretary at the YMCA during many of the years Daddy volunteered there.

Daddy was floored by the offer! He couldn't imagine having a desk job; he'd always done manual labor. As an uneducated black man born at the beginning of the twentieth century, he hadn't expected to do anything else. He was grateful to be healthy and strong enough to work steadily. At CAAP, he would not only make more money than he'd ever earned, but for the first time in his life, he'd wear a suit and tie to work. Paying off his mortgage would be a snap, and the heaviest thing he had to lift was a pen.

Daddy worked at CAAP for five years and loved every minute of it. When he retired at sixty-seven, he felt superfluous. Except for holidays and annual two-week vacations, he'd worked every day of his life since he was a child. Daddy didn't know what to do with himself without a job. His volunteer work had also tapered off over the years. With Mama's encouragement, Daddy had trained younger people to take over most of his church duties. Many of the neighborhood improvements he had lobbied for had been made, so what was next?

With little to do he seemed sad and his health began to fail. His physician advised us all to come home to see him for perhaps a final time in 1971, but Daddy rallied after telling me in the hospital, "The bible only promises us three score and ten." Daddy was referring to the tenth verse of Psalm 90, "The days of our years are threescore years and ten…." a verse he had often quoted. At Christmas of that year, he and Mama took their first airplane trip to visit me in California. The following summer, they drove to Delaware and visited my sister and her family, but by then Daddy had weakened and lost much of his customary cheerfulness. When Kamau, his last grandchild, was three months old, I took him to visit both sets of grandparents. Daddy held his spiritual heir in his arms a few months before he died in 1973. He had turned seventy four months earlier.

We were stunned. Although we knew Daddy wasn't well, we still did not believe he would die so young. Grandpa and his brothers—Daddy's uncles—had lived well past age eighty and we expected Daddy to do the same.

I couldn't stand it. I was thirty-six years old, but I was still "Daddy's girl" and the child in me believed him to be indestructible. What was I going to do now? He was the one person I always knew had my back. With him gone I felt exposed and unprotected.

Mama and Daddy had been married forty-six years. Because she didn't have any encouragement for her own dreams, Mama put her creative energies into flower gardening, making quilts, and encouraging her husband and children. She was sixty-seven when she lost her partner and the dynamic center of her life. She frequently reminisced about the work Daddy had done in the community where the family church was located. Mama worked closely with Daddy, and I had often heard them discussing what needed to be done, but she never asserted herself or sought credit for her efforts.

After Mama died, we found several pages she had written about Daddy's accomplishments at the church. I feel certain they were written near the end of her life, when cataracts had dimmed her vision, because her small, neat handwriting was larger than usual. Although the pages were numbered and stapled together, they were out of order and some were missing. Her writing was uncharacteristically repetitious with many misspelled words, but clearly it was a labor of love. She described in some detail his work with young people and how he built up the Sunday school at our church. She summarized in the following words.

"For many of these boys and girls he helped to get jobs, encouraged them to stay in school, go to college. If one of them got in trouble, he'd go to jail to see them, help them get a lawyer. If they were sent away to reform school, he'd visit them, pray for them, talk encouragingly. He met resentment from some of them; but pray[er] and faith kept him going."

When the *Indianapolis Recorder,* the black weekly newspaper, was preparing Daddy's obituary they called to question the information we had provided. The reporter said we hadn't mentioned where Daddy went to school. She was shocked to learn that his formal education ended at fourth grade. Daddy would have loved that his obituary and a large picture were on the front page of the **Recorder,** above the fold on September 29, 1973. Even the *Indianapolis Star,* the major daily paper, gave Daddy six inches with a picture on September 22. The week following the obituary, the *Recorder* ran an editorial about Daddy titled "One Man in Death." It said in part:

"Highly regarded throughout the city, he was a prime example of determination since all his civic and professional attainments were made without the benefit of formal education. … Future generations may make little note of Smith H. Cheatham and probably few today realize men of his caliber reside in Indianapolis. Aside from concerning himself with the support of a family, he found time to encourage the less determined and give relentless efforts toward bettering the community. …His legacy to the world: Try despite shortcomings."

"The Ballad of John Henry" reminds me of my daddy.

John Henry worked so hard
he broke his poor heart
and he laid down his hammer and he died.
Lawd, lawd,
He laid down his hammer and he died.

Link:

Recorder http://indiamond6.ulib.iupui.edu/cdm/compoundobject/collection/ IRecorder/id/53288/rec/79

✝

Never Failing To Protest

There may be times when we are powerless to prevent injustice, but there must never be a time when we fail to protest.
~ **Elie Wiesel**

This essay describes actual experiences. To avoid possible discomfort or litigation, I have changed and/ or satirized the names of some people and places.

"**YOU KNOW THE ONLY REASON** they hired you is because you're black."

"What are you talking about?"

"Lori in Sales told me that Detroit won't buy books from a company that doesn't have black editors."

"Well, if that's the case, they must be thrilled to have found *a black* as good as I am."

I turned my back to Sarah and ended the exchange. She stood there for a moment, then walked away from my cubicle.

The nerve of that stupid, white bitch! I had been a Ph.D. student at Stanford, worked for nearly five years as a state department curriculum consultant, *and* I've been published! And they hired me because I'm *black?!* She has a bachelor's and a couple of years editing manuals for a computer company. Did they hire her because she's white or Hungarian or whatever she is?

Sarah's resentment of me was visible and vicious. At a recent meeting while we waited for our manager to arrive, Sarah wondered aloud if it were true that Don (in sales, and rumored to be their top-seller) really did sleep with every female he traveled with. She was signifying because I had just returned from a presentation that included Don, although we had not traveled together. That ignorant bitch had had a burr in her butt since I was promoted to Editor I, leaving her behind as a II. What she didn't know was that I had to demand that promotion after I closed five of six sales in districts where the decision-makers were black.

She also didn't know, and would never learn from me, that, in fact, Don was a pimp for Ken Cooker, one of the corporate execs.

Cooker had a reputation (among the few black employees) for liking black women. It hadn't taken much for him to earn that sobriquet—he openly admired a black secretary who came to work in snug cocktail attire and garish costume jewelry, and he had taken Margie, the black woman in personnel, to lunch a couple of times.

After I had been with the company a couple of years, Don stopped by my cubicle one day. "Ken Cooker really likes your work."

"Good. I'm glad to hear it."

"You know, with your background, you could be Ken's executive assistant for multiculturalism."

"Who was the previous executive assistant for multiculturalism?"

"There's never been one; you would be the first. And it would pay a lot more."

When I didn't respond he said, "What d'ya think?"

"It sounds interesting, Don. Let me think about it."

I did think about it. For the first time, I owned a house by myself, which meant that I had to hire people for the yard work and anything else that needed doing or fixing. I could certainly use more money. But why was Don making this offer? Shouldn't Cooker have called me into his office and made the offer himself? A few days later, Don visited me again to learn my decision. I told him the truth.

"You know Don, I really enjoy being an editor, and I plan to one day become a senior editor. I don't think being Cooker's multicultural assistant would help with that."

"Really? Are you sure?" Don seemed surprised, but he didn't try to change my mind.

Either Cooker was not satisfied with my answer, or Don

decided to use another approach. A few days later, he was back in my office.

"You know you could really do well for yourself as Ken's assistant. You could double your salary, travel…." His voice trailed off. Then after a short pause, "Besides, you know Ken really likes black women."

There it was. I couldn't believe he had actually said it.

"Ken likes black women?" My voice rose with incredulity. "How can you tell? Where are the black women program managers? There are no blacks on the editorial board; only three black female professionals in the whole company and two of them, including me, are overqualified for their positions."

I stood up to look him in the face. "I *hope* you're not saying that Ken Cooker likes black women in the way white men *usually* like black women—behind closed doors with their legs open."

My outburst apparently killed Don's usual quick retort and smooth demeanor. He dropped his eyes and left my cubicle without another word. He never mentioned Ken Cooker to me again.

That night I went to Margie's house to play rise-and-fly bid whist, but I didn't consider telling her about Don's pimping for Ken Cooker. I had seen her flirting with Cooker, and I knew she also believed he had a weakness for black women. Although I hadn't played whist in years, a form of "beginner's luck" was with me because my partner and I sat for the whole evening; nobody could get us up. I even ran a "Boston."

I had been working in this crazed environment for nearly six years and had survived two "RIFs"(reductions in force). The corporate intrigue of competition for favor and promotions was making me physically ill. Every day on the drive to work, I got a headache. The pain had become routine, just like the job. When I was hired I thought I had found the career of my dreams. After a lifetime of longing, I had finally landed a job in book publishing. My first assignment was as an editor on the team doing a complete revision of the literature series. There were six textbooks for grades seven through twelve and each editor was responsible for two of these books.

It was a reader's fantasy come true: I was being *paid* to read books to find literary selections for an anthology. At first many of my selections were rejected as unsuitable. My experienced colleagues said the sales force would never approve them.

"Why not? Adolescents would love stories like this." I asked Rob, the program manager, to explain.

"They can't get them past C.A.R.P."

"What is 'C.A.R.P.'?"

"C.A.R.P. is the acronym for **C**itizen **A**ction for **R**esponsible **P**rograms. They monitor the textbook selection process in Bombasta and raise a huge fuss if a book has anything even slightly controversial."

"I know Bombasta is a big state, but why would an organization in *one* state influence what we put in the textbooks?"

"Bombasta is not only huge, but it chooses only a few texts in each subject for school districts to select from. If our books don't get on that short list, we can't sell there for five years."

"So? There are 49 other states."

"Yeah, but except for a few small states in the South, they're all open territory, which means our sales reps have to compete against every other textbook publisher. We do everything possible not to be closed out of Bombasta, including kow-towing to C.A.R.P."

C.A.R.P. was a small, self-righteous and vociferous group that went over textbooks line-by-line looking for and usually finding offensive ideas, words, pictures and concepts. Publishers had made expensive revisions in texts after an attack by C.A.R.P. The group knew precisely how to work people into a froth and grab media attention. In effect, C.A.R.P. controlled what went into textbooks sold all over the country. Consequently, we developed bland, insipid books that often failed to capture the attention of young people accustomed to the variety, light, sound and motion of television.

I found it difficult to believe that Dum & Down, or any publisher, would even try to produce a single textbook that appealed to every school system in the country—Alabama *and* Alaska, Maine *and* Mississippi, San Antonio *and* San Francisco. It made no sense to me. Despite the foolishness of the attempt, I was determined to find works by black, Hispanic, Native Americans and women authors that would pass their scrutiny.

Each textbook editor worked with Rob, the program manager; Oscar, the general "author" of the entire series; and a person who was designated the "author" of each text. These "authors" were selected because of their credentials. The editors did the bulk of the work and the authors signed off on it. Daniel was the author of the American Lit text I was editing. Dan was a born and bred New Englander and professor at a prestigious New England university. He and Oscar preferred to continue Dum & Down's tradition of a single-minded focus on, not only white authors, but *white males*, most of whom had lived and worked east of the Hudson River. Oscar and Dan, both older white men, didn't believe anyone else was on the level of the "classic writers."

I had been hired to help make all the books "multicultural," that is, to include the literature of groups that had traditionally been excluded from these texts. I decided to add more women as well. We all knew that was my assignment, but we often disagreed on the *type* of multicultural material. The rest of the team preferred innocuous "race-free" stories by black authors. Through sheer refusal to give up (they said I was stubborn, but I called it tenacious), I managed to get most of the writers and ideas I wanted. On one occasion when they were determined not to include something I wanted, I continued to argue for it.

"Let it go, Janet. You've been outvoted! It's time to give up," Rob tried to end the discussion because they all disagreed with me.

"I am *not outvoted*! The three of you represent only one perspective, that of older white men. I represent blacks, Native Americans, Hispanics, women and young people. You're outvoted!" (Actually, Rob was about my age, but he was white and male.)

And so, the finished American literature text included Benjamin Banneker's response to Thomas Jefferson's statement that blacks "could scarcely be found capable of comprehending Euclid," and the scene from Frederick Douglass's autobiography where he refused to allow the slave breaker to whip him. My colleagues wanted the passage where the slaveholder's wife begins teaching Douglass to read, but I wouldn't have it. I also added writers like Toni Morrison, Margaret Walker and N. Scott Momaday, whom they had never heard of, believe it or not.

I was surprised that Dan's fiercest resistance was to my recommendation to include excerpts from the Iroquois Constitution and mention that it was a model for the U.S. document. He was furious and indignant at the idea that the U.S. Constitution was not the exclusive brainchild of the British founding fathers. He relented only after I backed my claim by showing him articles and books by scholars he respected.

I insisted that Chinua Achebe, Derek Walcott and Mary Wollenstonecraft's "Vindication of the Rights of Women" be added to the massive, exclusively white and nearly all male British literature text. Charlie, the editor, was appalled at the suggestion that Achebe and Walcott be included.

"These people are not English."

"They're as English as William Butler Yeats."

Charlie just glared at me.

"Achebe and Walcott write in English for the same reason Yeats does: their countries, Nigeria, St. Kitts and Ireland, were all conquered by England."

To my deep dismay, one of the black authors I had fought hard to include denied us permission to excerpt her novel in a textbook. I couldn't believe it! After several attempts to contact her, I finally got her on the telephone. I explained who I was and why I was calling.

"I had to fight to persuade my co-workers that you *should* be included in our American Literature text, so I hope you will give us permission to use your work."

"I have no doubt you had to fight. I know how racist that publisher is, but the few times I've allowed my work to be anthologized, the editors have taken a snippet of something out of context, then written study questions that had nothing to do with the work. I'm not going to let that happen again."

"I can understand that, but please let me send you a copy of the selection we plan to use; I assure you it's not a snippet. And I'll write the instructional material myself and let you see that as well."

"I don't know…."

"Look, students are introduced to authors in their school texts. When they browse in bookstores they look for familiar names of authors they've read. We *have* to make sure that black authors are among those familiar names."

She agreed, but only under the condition that she approve the material before it was published. I had no problem with that.

The struggle to change those texts, and the challenges that provided were long past. Once the books were done, I helped train the sales reps on the content of the texts, and traveled on occasion to help close a few difficult deals. In one Midwestern school district, a member of the textbook selection committee chided us for not having enough black writers in the series. She recognized a couple of names—Langston Hughes and Richard Wright—but had I not been there, I doubt the sales reps would have known that Zora Neale Hurston, Mari Evans, Countee Cullen and Arna Bontemps were also black writers. I was appalled at the ignorance of the committee member but later remembered that the people who helped develop the textbooks hadn't known those writers either. Why would they? All of us—textbook authors, editors and educators—had received the same white-washed education, or *mis*-education as Carter G. Woodson put it.

I began working at Dum & Down Textbook Publishers in the late seventies. They hired me out of desperation because they had lost significant market share to competitors whom they had long considered low-class upstarts. Dum & Down was an old Highton company with the traditional Highton attitude: "If an idea didn't originate here or in Europe, it has no value." And its corollary: "If Hightonians don't know about it, it isn't worth knowing."

Their competitors had added a few blacks to their textbooks beginning in the early seventies; and as early as the late sixties some publishers had added a light brown tint to a couple of faces in their elementary readers. But Dum & Down, aside from hiring black sales reps for urban markets, had refused the lure of what they considered a passing fad and continued publishing text-books that rarely acknowledged the existence of anyone except east coast WASP males. When their bottom line began to redden, new management was brought in to stop the bleeding. The new guys first attended to what had been their best-selling reading series, then went to work on their line of secondary books. That's where I came in.

On my first day at work I noticed something peculiar. Charlie, who had been introduced as the program manager during my second interview, had been replaced. I eventually learned that Charlie had planned to hire someone else for my position—in his opinion a much better qualified white male. Because Charlie absolutely refused to have me on his team—not only was I black and female, I was from the Midwest—he was replaced by Rob. So Charlie, who had been with the company for nearly thirty years, was demoted from manager to senior editor, and in effect, we became peers, both reporting to Rob.

I liked working with Rob because once he gave me an assignment, he left me alone to complete it. If I had questions, he was helpful without being condescending.

A few months after I began my duties as an entry-level editor, Charlie wrote Rob a long memo about one of my assignments explaining how my lack of knowledge was apparent in my work. Charlie laid out a meticulously detailed case explaining why I was not qualified to be a textbook editor. Much of it was a petty display of Charlie's pique over the new multicultural direction of the program, but he also pointed out some editing mistakes. When Rob passed the memo on to me without comment, I assumed that meant he agreed with Charlie's diatribe. In my written response to Rob I asked why Charlie had been examining my work since that was Rob's job. I made it clear that I would not consider any evaluation of my assignments unless it came from my manager. Rob did not defend Charlie, nor did he want to chastise his former boss, so he dropped the matter without a word. I never saw another evaluation from Charlie. Privately, I found some of Charlie's points useful and applied them to my work.

Charlie was sixty-something and quite proud to have spent his entire life in New England. He found little of value outside his native area, except in Europe. He considered the literature program to be his, having nurtured it for decades, and now it was being taken apart before his eyes and there was nothing he could do about it. I was the only black in the vicinity, so, in the time-honored American tradition, Charlie made me his scapegoat. In the nearly three years we worked together he never acknowledged or spoke to me unless the work demanded it, and then he would be either caustic or patronizing. My first instinct was to regard Charlie as a racist pig, but after giving it some thought, I concluded that possibly for the first time in his professional life, Charlie was powerless. He couldn't prevent me from being hired or stop the revision of the program. Plus there was no way to get rid of me. Charlie's surly attitude was an indication of his impotence. He had resorted to hating me, which in the words of Howard Thurman was "the last great fortress of the weak."

The corporate attitude toward blacks, however, was a more

serious matter. At Dum & Down we were to be seen and not heard. I was weary of having to fight for the consideration and promotions that were routinely offered to white men and to a select few, usually attractive and flirtatious, white women. After five years and using every tactic I could think of short of a lawsuit, I finally made senior editor. By then, Charlie had retired, Rob had accepted a generous severance package, and Sarah had been transferred to another department. Now there were rumors that the company might be sold, which undoubtedly meant there would be more RIFs. Apparently, the multicultural effort had been too little, too late, or maybe that was never the problem. Dum & Down was a small division of a large multinational corporation that demanded profits, not excuses.

I was put in charge of the literature program. With only clerical assistance and without the title of program manager, I contracted for the art and made the editorial revisions necessary to update the copyright on all six books. When the editorial board made the decision to add a consumable testing program to the series, I interviewed, hired and supervised the freelance writers. I also corrected and sometimes wrote marketing copy and trained the sales staff on program changes.

One day, Jim, the company's publisher, brought Oscar, the general author of the lit series, to my office. I had not seen Oscar since we completed the revision, but I knew he and Jim were long-time friends.

Jim smiled broadly as he entered my low-walled space. "Hi, Janet. Oscar's back; he's been hired full-time to manage the literature series and you'll be working for him. Bring him up to speed on what you've been doing with it."

THUD! My heart sank as I received the blow. I was to train Oscar to be my boss.

In that moment I *accepted* the reality of my situation. *This is the way it has been, is and will be. I have to fight for every inch of ground I gain.*

Of course, I could have fought this latest humiliation—sued them for sexism and racism, but that would indicate I wanted to continue an association with them, but I'd had enough of Dum & Down. Not only that, but after mulling over this latest turn of events, I had a revelation. If I worked as hard for myself as I had for them, I could be successful as my own boss.

My final act of protest was to take charge of my life and create my own employment. Less than a year after Oscar was hired, I resigned, suddenly, or so they thought.

Making Changes, Being Changed

All that you touch,
You Change

All that you Change,
Changes you.

~ Octavia E. Butler in Parable of the Sower

ONE DAY I STOOD UP FROM my desk and looked around at the maze of low-walled cubicles and pondered my frustration with my employer. In that moment I had a flash of intuition. *I need to get out of here and do something else!*

I was sick of my job—the corporate politics and dog-eat-dog scrambling for promotions—and I wasn't happy with where I lived; my home had been burglarized twice in the past year. Perhaps it was possible to actually *enjoy* myself while I earned a living. If I work as hard for myself as I've worked for this corporation, I thought, I should be able to succeed as my own boss. There was only one way to find out. From that moment on I made plans for my son and me to take the road "less traveled by." That moment of clarity led to my creating new products and making unexpected contributions to the book industry.

I was forty-six years old in December 1983 when I began plotting my escape. Seven months later I officially quit my job as a textbook editor in a Boston suburb, and left what for me was a cold, unwelcoming place. As another declaration of my autonomy, I was deliberate about selecting where I wanted to live. Every place I'd lived up to that point had been chosen for me by my parents, a husband, or a job. Growing up in Indianapolis, I'd visited Chicago many times and, although I didn't have friends or relatives in the city, I was acquainted with a couple of people there. More important, unlike Boston, where I never felt comfortable, I felt welcome in Chicago, that huge, exciting, world-class city. The fact that it was a short two and a half hour drive from home and my aging mother made it even more appealing. I was also attracted by the idea of living in a place where there were lots of black people and black cultural activity; a city where a black was actually running the place. Harold Washington had just taken office as Chicago's mayor.

Once I settled on what I wanted, everything required to make it happen tumbled into place *just as I needed it*. Not long after I'd picked Chicago, my employer sent me there on business *two times*. I added vacation days to each trip and looked for a place to live. I found a three-bedroom condo in a vintage three-story brick six-flat walk-up, in Hyde Park, a few blocks from the University of Chicago. (Hyde Park is a college town located in the middle of a major city.) The second-floor unit had been rehabbed throughout with new appliances. The previous owners had stripped decades of paint and varnish from the oak floors, woodwork, and an elegant carved mantel over a defunct fireplace. The entryway had a built-in mirror with coat hooks, and the living room looked out on a neighborhood park on the other side of the street. I arranged to buy it, and returned home to put my Boston house up for sale.

I was unprepared for the immediate offer—at the asking price—from the first person who looked at my house. The prospective buyer wanted it right away. I wasn't going to move before my eleven-year-old son Kamau completed the school year, so I didn't accept the offer. My realtor was furious at the loss of a quick sale and declined to work with me any further. I was actually relieved at her decision because we had disagreed on the asking price. She would only list the house at a price she determined, insisting that as an "experienced realtor" she knew what the market would bear. In other words, what I wanted was irrelevant. When I turned down the offer, she was done with me. A couple of months later I found another realtor who was skeptical, but at least willing to list the house at forty percent more than I'd paid for it five years earlier. (I'm not sure why, but I recognized the early inflation of the housing bubble.) Again, offers were quick in coming and the house sold at slightly less than the increased asking price. After Kamau left to spend his usual summer with his dad, I completed the sale and packed to move. By August 1984 I was settled in Chicago.

As eager as I was to be my own boss, I was also nervous about it. Despite my savings and the windfall from selling the house, I wasn't sure how I would *keep* the cash flowing, especially since I didn't receive a penny of child support. For grades two through six, Kamau had attended a prestigious private school in Brookline, a suburb contained wholly within Boston's borders. I called it prudence, but I was so scared, that in Chicago I enrolled him in a public school. He hated it. In sharp contrast to his Brookline school it was an antiquated, dismal place with large classes and obsolete textbooks. For Kamau, Chicago was a strange place where he didn't have any friends. He was miserable, and no doubt also absorbed my anxiety about where money would come from now that I was no longer employed. He asked to go live with his father; at least he knew people in Mobile. His dad was eager to have him so I made the agonizing decision to let him go. I knew he would spend summers with me, but still, I missed him so much that sometimes my chest literally ached. With the clarity of hindsight, I can see that early puberty was the perfect time for him to be with his male parent. When Kamau left he was about three inches shorter than my five-feet-five inches. He was taller and lankier when he returned home. In the two and a half years he lived in Mobile—until the end of ninth grade—he literally grew a foot, twelve inches! By the time he got back I was more confident in my ability to keep the cash flowing, and he enrolled in high school at the University of Chicago Lab School.

DO WHAT YOU LOVE

Before I left Boston, my electronics guru friend, Alvin Foster, suggested I take advantage of the dramatically lowered price on a Commodore computer. (I think that model was being discontinued). I ordered the computer to be sent to my new residence for my home office. It came with a dot matrix printer and reams of paper. This was long before computers were user-friendly, and I knew absolutely nothing about them. Fortunately, another tech-savvy friend, Sam Williams who was visiting Chicago, helped me set the new computer up and connect everything. I was all set up and ready to fulfill my childhood dream of writing and publishing books—though I didn't yet have the courage to call myself a writer or publisher.

I cannot put into words what a magnificent feeling it was (and still is) to be free to organize my time and do with it as I please. As much as I missed Kamau's joy and affection, I soon recognized that without him there, I was less anxious and had time to figure out how to proceed. I could also accept the consulting gigs offered by my former employer that required me to travel throughout the country. I enjoyed flying around at someone else's expense. To meet people of like mind and shared interests, I joined a couple of professional groups—The Chicago Book Clinic and Chicago Women in Publishing. My life was so delicious, I felt embarrassed. I'd been taught to think of life largely as an obligation to be endured with only occasional moments of pleasure. Most of your time was spent working, the drudgery required to get the money you needed to eat and pay the bills. I had to learn not to feel guilty about loving what I was doing.

In between consulting trips, I put together a manuscript of quotations I had been collecting for a few years. At just the right moment, the Chicago Book Clinic put on their biennial PubTech, a trade show for book publishers. It turned out to be a great investment. I attended workshops on the various aspects of putting a book together, including how to price them (whatever the market will bear). At the vendors' exhibits, I found a printer whose specialty was manufacturing the pocket-size (3 ½" x 5 ½") book that I preferred. I introduced myself to the one other black person at the trade show, other than my sometime employee Vinita Ricks and me. He was a book designer named M. Earle Pitts. While the three of us had a drink I told him why we were there. He asked if I had a designer. I did not. I had written to a book designer friend in Boston about my project, but he had not responded. Earle, a big-time $300-an-hour New York designer, offered to design my book at no charge! I jumped at the chance and sent him the manuscript right away. (Talk about things falling into place. Wow!) Later he told me he'd made the same offer to other black self-publishers, but I was the first to take him up on it. He also gave me valuable tips on dealing with the trade book market advising me to take books to the annual American Booksellers Association (ABA) national convention, now called Book Expo America. He also suggested that I advertise in *Publishers Weekly*. I did both.

I established Sabayt (pronounced SAH-be-aht) Publications to publish my first book, *Famous Black Quotations and some not so famous* in 1986. ("Sabayt" is a transliteration of ancient Egyptian hieroglyphics meaning "to transfer wisdom; gain understanding.") Before I invested in publishing my manuscript, I checked the massive Bowker publications, *Books in Print* and *Subject Guide to Books in Print,* to see if there were any similar books already on the market. These huge tomes listed 151 quotation collections on myriad topics including golf, business, Italians, and Jews, but not one on blacks/Negroes/African Americans. I knew lots of black people who would welcome a book of our quotations, especially if it was small enough to fit into a pocket or purse. I decided to go for it.

I took a huge risk and ordered a first printing of 5,000 copies, not realizing that it was an appallingly large initial print run for a novice self-publisher. However, my desire to significantly cut the unit cost was more important to me than being practical. They wouldn't go out of date and I figured I'd sell them eventually. What I hadn't thought about was where I would *store* so many books. I panicked when I was asked that question. Again, serendipitously, my friend Alvin came to my rescue. He had recently moved his business into a large building with tons of vacant space, some of which he planned to rent out. Not only that, but he operated a direct mail service! I had a couple of boxes of the first printing shipped to my home, and the rest were delivered to Alvin's warehouse. Alvin instructed me on how to process the orders. When I received an order, I typed an address label and a packing slip, sent them to Alvin, and he shipped the books out. Good thing I still had my typewriter since the computer wasn't capable of producing individual labels and forms in triplicate.

On the blank pages at the end of my seventy-one page book I printed order forms. To my delight, lots of people used them! I also mailed complimentary copies of *Famous Black Quotations* to influential people like Earl Graves at *Black Enterprise* and Susan Taylor at *Essence*. Both responded with letters of praise for *Famous Black Quotations,* and I used statements from those letters in promotional material. I sent a comp copy as well to Richard Morgan, then president of Scott Foresman & Company, textbook publishers. Dr. Morgan had been editor-in-chief of the publisher I worked for in Boston. He gave me the best endorsement of all— an order for 2,000 copies. He used the book as a gift from his company to the attendees at a National Alliance of Black School Educators conference. Although *Famous Black Quotations* had been in print only six months, I had less than a thousand copies left; not enough to fill Scott Foresman's order.

I needed a second printing!

AND THE MONEY WILL FOLLOW

My promotional efforts along with Earle's important suggestions had led to brisk sales. I had taken my hot-off-the-press book to New Orleans, site of the ABA convention in 1986. In addition to sharing booth space with another self-publisher, Vinita and I took turns walking the convention floor giving books to every black person and to anybody wearing a booksellers' badge. I also collected business cards from bookstores for a mailing list. Several booksellers placed orders on the spot. I left the convention having secured book stores to sell *Famous Black Quotations* all across the country and contact information for a host of other potential customers.

One of Mayor Washington's objectives was to amend Chicago's slogan "The City That Works," to "The City That Works *Together*," the implication being that the city would work not only for white males, but for everybody. City departments were mandated to include ethnic minorities and women among their business vendors. The Midwestern Division of Baker & Taylor Books (B & T), a national wholesale distributor that serviced hundreds of libraries, had provided books to the Chicago Public Library for years. The library informed B & T they needed to include minority vendors as a part of their business if they wanted to continue as their book supplier. And this is where Earle's second suggestion led to even wider distribution of *Famous Black Quotations.*

Earle told me to put an ad in *Publishers Weekly* announcing both the publication of my book and my presence at ABA. Baker & Taylor, located in Momence, Illinois, saw the ad and contacted me to explore the possibility of our working together. In true Chicago style, B & T had been approached by a couple of politically connected Chicagoans offering to guarantee the library contract by pretending to be their minority vendor, for a fee. Fortunately for me, Baker & Taylor turned them down to look for an actual vendor. When B & T read the *Publishers Weekly* ad for *Famous Black Quotations* (a clue that it might be a black business), and saw that I was located in Chicago, they contacted me. They did not pull any punches at our first meeting, telling me immediately that their interest in me was in response to the city's mandate. They also told me about their encounter with the guys who offered to front for them. They weren't exactly sure what I could do for them, but at least I was a legitimate minority business. I knew what they could do for me. I asked them to stock and distribute my book, and they agreed. What a coup! I would guess that B & T had never before set up an account for a self-publisher with one title. Libraries and bookstores around the country would learn about my book and could and did include it in their Baker & Taylor orders.

I also had an idea about how B & T and I could work together. We were some twenty years beyond the paradigm-shifting civil rights movement of the sixties. By the late eighties we were into the period when African Americans were slowly being phased into places where we had traditionally been kept out—the corporate world, supervisory and management positions in various arenas, and election to public office at nearly all levels. In addition, encouraged by these new opportunities, blacks were attending college in record numbers. Black bookstores, including some black bookstore chains, had sprouted all over the country. I knew these stores were interested primarily, if not exclusively, in books written by and about African Americans. However, though more such books were being published, they were hard to find. Often they were published by boutique presses, black publishers, and university presses with little marketing clout. Unless the author was a celebrity, the major houses were not investing much money in promoting the few black books they occasionally published. The publishing industry, like the rest of America, paid scant attention to the doings of anybody outside what they considered the "mainstream," which was a euphemism for "white folks with disposable income."

As a consultant to Baker & Taylor I suggested they gather these marginalized titles into a catalog. That way bookstores and librarians could easily locate the titles they wanted. We started by sponsoring a two-day Minority Book Expo at the Chicago Public Library featuring books by and about African Americans, Hispanic Americans, Native American Indians and Asian Americans. I don't remember all the details, but according to the *Publishers Weekly* coverage of December 26, 1986, we requested information on such books from three hundred publishers and one hundred replied. We had over a thousand titles on display. I convened a panel at the expo that included representatives from Chicago's black publishers to discuss the black book publishing industry. I invited Dr. Nicholas Kanellos, professor of Hispanic and classical languages at the University of Houston, to speak to the gathering—Nick and I had worked together at the Indiana Department of Education about ten years earlier. Elizabeth Nunez, a professor at Medgar Evers College in Brooklyn, NY, whose novel *When Rocks Dance* had just been published, was also a speaker.

In May of the following year, Baker & Taylor sponsored another Multi-Cultural Book Expo in Southfield, Michigan, just outside Detroit, and asked me to be the featured speaker. Later in 1987 I developed, and Baker & Taylor published, their first annotated listing of books by and about African Americans. B & T distributed the catalog to their bookstore and library customers around the country and they began using it. We updated it each year through 1989. With Nick Kanellos' help, in 1989 we added the *Hispanic Bibliography of the U.S.* By then the bibliographies were so successful—growing their business by twenty-five percent I was told—that B & T's national office took it over so that all their divisions could be involved. Soon competing wholesalers began publishing their own catalogs of African American titles.

LEARNING FROM MISTAKES

Since my book was selling so well, I decided to develop a *Famous Black Quotations* calendar. The only black history calendars I had seen were the ones produced by beer and liquor companies in the sixties, and they hadn't been around for a while. I thought there were probably people who would like their black history straight, without ads. The first *Famous Black Quotations Wall Calendar* was published in 1988 and I added it to the B & T bibliography. Aesthetically, the calendar was plain; its primary appeal was that there was no similar calendar available. The art was black and white pen drawings by Buck Brown, who had been a cartoonist and illustrator for *Playboy* back in the day. Each page featured a portrait and quotation by a black person important in our history—like Sojourner Truth, Marcus Garvey, Paul Robeson, Mary McLeod Bethune—and a brief biography of that person. I ordered way too many of them, but sold enough to cover the costs, then gave away what remained, mostly to the Chicago public schools, who seemed happy to get them.

Each consecutive year I had to invest more money to make the calendars a little fancier. At the same time sales were dropping because every year there was more competition, and their calendars were slicker than mine. Fortunately, I had consulting clients like Scott Foresman; Tradery House, publishers of *The Black Family Reunion Cookbook;* and Baker & Taylor to keep me going, because the calendars were chewing up my bottom line. The short sales period for calendars and the flashy four-color competition made me give up the calendars after four years. I should have stopped after the second year, but I mistakenly thought adding color would save me. I learned the hard way that books are a far better investment than calendars.

I'd had repeated requests for another book of quotations, so in 1992, instead of spending money on another calendar, I published *Famous Black Quotations on Women, Love and other topics.* The new book had the same trim size and design, with a red rather than blue cover, but it was twenty-five pages longer than the first collection. Working alone for the most part, except for Kamau's help when he was in Chicago, I sold over 90,000 copies of the two titles between 1986 and 1994. Sales were strong enough that I primarily serviced wholesalers and sent Alvin orders only for cartons of books. On occasion I accepted a smaller order that I shipped myself. The second book invigorated sales, but I was growing weary of taking orders, typing labels and invoices, and collecting from customers. What I wanted to do most was write more books. After several rejections, I finally found a literary agent willing to present my books to major publishers in the hope that one of them would take over publishing my titles. She found two New York publishers who made offers. I was expecting far more money than either publisher offered and turned the offers down. The agent was able to get a small increase from one publisher, but I still balked and although she tried, she couldn't convince me to accept the offer. Finally, she refused to represent me any longer with the words, "You self-publishers always think your stuff is worth so much more than it is."

I resigned myself to continue publishing the books on my own. A few weeks later, I received a call from Colleen Kapklein, an editor at Warner Books. She had followed up with the agent about the offer and been told I turned it down. She asked the agent if she could contact me directly and the agent had no problem with that because she refused to represent "difficult" people like me. I told Colleen I wanted more money than Warner had initially offered. She asked a question the agent never had: "How much do you want?" I told her and the next day she called back to say that Warner agreed to pay what I asked. I licensed both titles to Warner, added a number of new quotations, and they combined the two books into one 4 ½" x 6" volume of 144 pages titled simply *Famous Black Quotations*.

Warner's edition of *Famous Black Quotations* published in 1995 was the third in what became for me a series of ten collections of quotations by people of African descent. (All of my books are listed in the back of this book.) Eleven years earlier when I decided to engage in my pursuit of happiness, I had no idea what would happen, but I was willing to take the risk.

It has been a life-changing adventure during which I've made mistakes and had periods of severe anxiety. But I also discovered how resourceful I could be in crisis situations, something I never could have learned working for someone else and following orders. I can see now that all my experiences have been part of the process of discovering who I am and what I'm capable of doing. I still love what I do.

✦
Writing for Myself and Hoping

*Better to write for yourself and have no public, than
to write for the public and have no self.*
~ Cyril Connolly

A response to *New York Times* op-ed columns:
"Would the Bard Have Survived the Web?"
and
"The Slow Death of the American Author"

I AM A MEMBER AND ADMIRER of the Authors Guild, and I understand why the Guild continues to challenge the new technology that is transforming the book publishing industry as we have known it. Change is always difficult, and especially so for those who prosper under the crumbling status quo. This new digital age, however, is better for me. It is democratizing institutions that have long been controlled by a powerful few who decided who and what got published, and which books would be heavily promoted. As we learn to navigate these uncertain possibilities, of course, there will be mistakes and excesses, but the future is now and I choose to explore the new path rather than fight it.

Amazon and Google are the "villains" in this divide, publishing houses the "heroes," and writers allegedly the victims. As a writer who has both self-published and been published by major companies, I am one of the alleged victims. However, I am not threatened by Amazon and Google, greedy behemoths though they may be, because I am not a profit-making corporation. I see these companies as hatchets chopping away at the mammoth icebergs that have controlled the passage between creative artists and their audiences. I am happier for the greater exposure Amazon and Google provide for my work than I am concerned about abuses of copyright law or books being "held hostage." I know I live in a capitalist culture where "property" is nearly as sacred as life itself, and in some cases more so, but I want my "property" to reach as many eyes as possible.

Major publishers have to satisfy stockholders and burnish bottom lines and that has always left "midlist" writers like me starving for attention and royalties. We "midlisters" don't have much to lose from changes in the industry. Who knows, this may be the best thing that's happened for us in a long time. My early experimenting with the new technology is revealing. I have received more royalties from a self-published e-book that's been available less than a year, than I have from a hardcover of the same title that's been on the market for seven years. And that's not to mention how long I have to wait for the hardcover publisher to deliver those few dollars.

I do understand why best selling authors are disturbed; they actually get rich from their books—by sales to readers and/or from movie options. They could possibly lose significant income. However, some of us are writing more for satisfaction than remuneration—writing primarily for the love of it because the big bucks have not been forthcoming. As one of those writers, I am not panicked that someone may copy a passage from one of my books and share it with other readers. The more people who find what I write compelling enough to share, the better I like it.

There are others who feel the same way I do. In the summer of 2014, several well-known and best-selling authors **protested an action by Amazon** that they said was "harming the livelihood of the authors on whom it has built its business." Interestingly, several self-published writers **started a petition** that came to Amazon's defense.

Many of the twelve books I've had published are now out of print. I intend to republish some of my titles because a market still exists for them, just not enough of a market to matter to the corporate publishing industry. By using the new technology to print copies as they are requested (Publish-on-Demand), I can sell books via my website so long as I want. Or sell them as downloads to e-readers. My first book was self-published in 1986. At that time, established publishers were not interested in my subject matter. Even without the Internet and POD, I sold more copies of the books I published myself than any major publisher ever sold of the titles they brought out. From that experience, I concluded that no other producer of my work will be as passionate about promoting my books as I am. Now that technological advances have made it easier, not only to produce books, but also to access potential customers, I am delighted.

I write to discover who I am and then to share what I've discovered with as many people as are interested. In the words of my favorite writer, James Baldwin, my writing may hurt or offend my readers, "but in order for me to do it, it had to hurt me first. I can only tell you about yourself as much as I can face about myself." I'd also like to think that my writing does what Baldwin says it should: "excavate the experience of the people who produced [me]."

The new technology will open more opportunities for many writers and encourage folks who have never written a book to tell their stories. The digital era has increased opportunities for entertainers, journalists, and political dissenters to find their particular audiences, and it can do the same for writers. In an experiment, the comedian **Louis C.K.** produced a brand-new standup special and made it easy as possible to buy, download and enjoy, free of any restrictions. Louie wondered, "[Will] everyone just go and steal it? Will they pay for it? And how much money can be made by an individual in this manner?" Not only did he cover his costs; he made a profit!

The first people to feel the pinch as technology creates these new openings are not the creative artists, but the people in the middle who have controlled the artists' access to their audiences and, consequently, to their money. Eventually (and that could mean within the coming decade), most artists will create their work and sell it directly to their audiences either via the Internet or as they speak and/or perform before live groups. Seems promising to me.

Links:

"Would the Bard Have Survived the Web?" in *N.Y. Times*, February 15, 2011
http://www.nytimes.com/2011/02/15/opinion/15turow.html?module=Search&ma bReward=relbias%3Ar&_r=0 `

"The Slow Death of the American Author"
http://www.nytimes.com/2013/04/08/opinion/the-slow-death-of-the-american-author.html?pagewanted=1&_r=1

protested an action by Amazon http://www.authorsunited.net/

started a petition
https://www.change.org/petitions/hachette-stop-fighting-low-prices-and-fair-wages

Louis C.K. https://buy.louisck.net/news/a-statement-from-louis-c-k

Looking Forward with Aging Grace

No matter how old you are there's always something good to look forward to.

~ Lynn Johnson

THIS ESSAY IS ABOUT ME, a woman who wasn't born yesterday; who was, in fact, born before 1940; a woman who is no longer looking for Mr. Right or Mr. Wrong. The significant issues for me now are staying healthy, parenting a grown child, learning to be a good mother-in-law and grandparent, coping with losses and change, living alone and aging.

Most challenging is accepting the mounting losses—of parents, siblings, husbands, friends, a dependent child, and the vitality I once had in spades. I grew up in a home with both parents, a sister and two brothers, and my aunt and same-age cousin just two houses away. These were the intimate relationships that shaped and informed my childhood. Nobody else is familiar with the events, people and places of those long-ago days, but every member of my childhood family is now deceased! The last remaining family members of my youth were my younger brother and my widowed brother-in-law, who joined the family fifty years ago when I was a young woman. The two of them died the same week, rudely ripping away the final physical ties to my roots.

There's no one left with whom to check my early memories. When I recently discovered that our childhood home had been torn down, immediately I wanted to share the news, but with whom? I miss my family members' physical presence, especially talking to them, but I am reminded by their offspring and my memories that they are still with me. Indeed, on occasion I've received direct communication from one or the other of them, sometimes in dreams, but also when I'm awake. I anticipated that as I aged my interest in some things would change and I'd have less energy perhaps, but I never once thought about losing *every close family member* with whom I'd shared my youth. I'm finding it difficult to reconcile this loss. I realize now that the longer you live, the more funerals you attend, but I'm not ready to die.

Nor am I going to deny my age. The only time I ever lied about my age, I was twelve pretending to be fourteen. Since then I haven't hesitated to tell anyone who wants to know how old I am. And by any measure, I'm an elder now, or if you prefer euphemisms, call me a senior citizen or seasoned citizen. A friend once said that I gleefully tell my age because I look much younger. Maybe. But I like to think I look younger because my life keeps getting better as I get older. I don't resist aging and I don't feel old.

I'm in my eighth decade and more comfortable with myself than I have ever been. I am actually joyful most of the time, something that seemed to elude me when I was younger. This deep satisfaction comes from finally being *conscious* of what I'm doing and knowing and accepting *who I am*. Acceptance of myself has been life-altering. I spent far too much of my life in self-criticism. For many years I had jarring emotional reactions to triggers that I wasn't conscious of and certainly didn't understand. Something was never quite right, so I was always on the move: leaving home, leaving husbands, changing jobs, moving to another part of the country. What I needed was to be still and listen to myself, but I didn't know that. My wanderings were useful, however; each change brought me closer to self-knowledge and finally back to what I was born to do—write.

Perhaps I never feared aging because of my unconventional paternal grandmother, whom I admired. She wasn't interested in "women's work." She labored in the tobacco field alongside her husband and sons and left the cooking and housework to her daughters. When I visited my grandparents, Grandpa was the one who cooked—he had to if he wanted to eat. I also applaud the way she left this earth. Without being ill, she went to sleep one night and didn't rise the next morning. (Daddy said she was never sick.)

As a child I loved nothing more than seeing impeccably coiffed salt-and-pepper hair topping off an elegant wardrobe. If the woman also had a career and traveled across the country or around the world, I was even more impressed. These women of the world were the opposite of my mother, whose life focused primarily on child-rearing, household duties, husband and church. Although my mother promoted her lifestyle as the one I should aspire to, I never did. I wanted a career and a child. I did not want to be a housewife, or a wife, for that matter. I would have welcomed a loving partnership with an intelligent, capable man, but the men of my generation had no model for that. I'm sure there were some who would have welcomed an equal partner, but I wasn't emotionally healthy enough to attract such a man, or astute enough to recognize him if he had walked into my life. It took a long time for me to become comfortable living my life the way that most fulfilled me.

At this age, I feel like a member of an exclusive club—the gray-haired, wise, curious, enthusiastic, vigorous, long-lived women. I'd prefer all-white hair, but I'm content with my white highlights. I have less stamina than when I was younger; if I stay up until midnight, there's no chance I will be raring to go at six, or even eight, in the morning. That loss of endurance, however, is more than compensated for by my increased savvy about ways to conserve energy. Dust can remain in my house for weeks before I feel compelled to wipe it away. I'm careful about what I eat, so I cook my own meals, rarely eating out. But I only cook three or four times a month, freeze small portions and eat what some might call leftovers, but I'm well-nourished and astoundingly healthy.

The best conservation of energy, however, comes from the five "happy life rules" I've devised. The first is that I say, "No, thank you. I have other plans," to invitations I don't relish. This has saved me untold remorse. On the occasions when I've allowed myself to ignore this rule, I literally have emotional convulsions that remind me if I want to be happy, I must be true to myself. The second is being content with whatever I'm able to do. When I do say "yes" to something, I no longer have any anguish about whether or not I'm doing "enough." I am satisfied with my best effort whether anybody else is pleased or not.

Although it may not be immediately evident, my next two rules go together. The first one I heard from a motivational speaker on public television, but the more I thought about it, the better I liked it. He said, "It's none of your business what other people think of you." Carolyn Myss stated it another way that had an even more profound impact on me in her book *Sacred Contracts*. She wrote, "When you do not seek or need external approval, you are at your most powerful." The time (and energy) I've saved by not being concerned about what "they" will think has allowed me to indulge another happy life rule—doing something just because I want to, whether it's sensible or productive or not.

My fifth rule, to let my grown child *be*, may be the most important because it helps me have a spectacular relationship with my son. Like most moms, I longed to put my child in a bubble that would shield him from disappointment and pain. Since that's not possible, we parents wind up trying to talk our children out of making mistakes. That doesn't work either. All it does is create hard feelings between you and your child. My son wasn't having it anyway, so I had to give it up. It's a work-in-progress, but he's training me to parent an adult child. It hasn't been easy for him because I was totally ignorant of the correct way to do this. There are lots of books on parenting growing children, but the books on parenting *grown* children didn't come out until after my training was well underway.

What I knew about parenting an adult child I got from my mother's relationship with me. And though I detested the fact that she was still instructing me at age forty as if I were ten, I often heard her speak when I was talking to my son. When that happened early in my training, my son interrupted and said something like: "Ma, I know how to do this; I do it all the time when you're not here." That was usually enough to jog me into consciousness and the realization I was doing the exact thing I hated from my own mother. I didn't say this out loud because my son adored his grandmother and doesn't take kindly to criticisms of her, implied or otherwise. On other occasions when I was visiting him, he sometimes needed to remind me that we were in his house, so *his* rules applied, not mine.

Because I have been blessed with a loving and considerate child, his corrections are gentle, not hostile, unlike my own attempts to change my mother's behavior. I never feel attacked when he points out my inappropriate comments, just acutely embarrassed. I had promised myself repeatedly that I would never, ever talk to my adult child the way Mama had talked to me. The recognition that I was doing exactly that etched a deep lesson on my heart.

I've zipped my lips and he learns from his own mistakes, which would have happened anyway; mistakes are the most effective teacher. Occasionally my mouth flies open before I've engaged my brain, but most of the time, no matter what he's going through, I do not offer advice. If he specifically asks for direction, which is rare, more often than not I say, "Follow your heart."

My son has no illusions about parental perfection or infallibility because I admit when I'm wrong and apologize when necessary. That way he knows it's not a disaster when he missteps. Admonishing him no longer crosses my mind. Consequently, he is open and candid with me. For a long time, until he met his wife, I was his best friend and we are still close. Another benefit of accepting the fact that my son is an intelligent, capable adult man is that I worry less and sleep better.

He and his wife have presented me with two precious and truly amazing granddaughters who add even more joy to my life.

Watching them develop into twenty-first century women is an exciting prospect and gives me one more thing to look forward to.

Life keeps getting better.

Seeking

Spiritual Power

Looking for God

*The nature of God is a circle of which the center is every-
where and the circumference is nowhere.*

~ Empedocles

I HAVE ABANDONED MY CHILDHOOD BELIEF that God is an ancient, bearded white male who resides above the sky and directs
the earth's people and all the action. (As a black woman I can't
wrap my mind around the idea of being ordered about by a white
man. I guess it's racial memory or something.) I've explored several different religions but found most to be similar to fraternities
and sororities: exclusive organizations requiring initiation rites
and professions of loyalty as prerequisites for membership. Once
the entry rites into these restrictive clubs are fulfilled, members
are obligated to participate in additional rituals to remain in
good standing. As with nearly all institutions, the goal of many
religious organizations is to grow as large as possible which, of
course, requires diligent and ongoing proselytizing. Other religions, however, have such rigid rules that only a tiny fraction of
the people in the world meeting certain conditions are acceptable
to their God.

These types of institutions have no appeal for me because I've
come to perceive God as inclusive of everyone and everything in
the universe, without qualifications and with no exceptions. But,
where is God? And who is God?

A scientist once told me that we humans created God to
explain things we observed—like thunderstorms, hurricanes,
tornadoes, earthquakes—but whose causes we didn't understand,
and this seems plausible. These powerful events wreak havoc
and severely damage human constructions, so whatever made
them happen had to be very powerful. Humans have also needed

God to allay our fear of catastrophic events as well as illness and death. We also needed to understand the life-sustaining abundance in our environment—plants grew that we and animals could eat. And we could hunt and eat the animals. No matter how much we ate, the plants and animals were replenished. New people were born that kept our societies going even though everybody eventually died. Obviously there was an enormous intelligence behind all this. Some human societies egocentrically decided that only a human—like us, but with more power—could have organized things so precisely. Once we decided God was a person, we were compelled to give that person an identity and personality. Amazingly, the Judeo/Christian religion configured God as an insecure older man who insists upon being placated and flattered, and, who knows, if we flatter God enough, that might stave off the earthquakes. Some religions decided that this anxious old man saw us as disgraceful sinners who are obviously unworthy of His attention because we are nothing and God is All.

If God indeed created man in his own image, why would he then disapprove of his own creation, or be so perverse as to punish his works unless they praise, cajole or plead with him? It seems oxymoronic to me that God has an inferiority complex that needs to be pumped up by constant praise. It is also incredible that an unstable old man with petty human frailties created this complex and glorious universe we live in.

And besides, in whose image were women created?

In his book, *Proof of Heaven: A Neurosurgeon's Journey into the Afterlife*, Eben Alexander sums up what many who claim near-death experiences have said, "[Most] of what people have had to say about God and the higher spiritual worlds has involved bringing them down to our level, rather than elevating our perceptions up to theirs. We taint, with our insufficient descriptions, their truly awesome nature."

Although I was raised in Indiana, my family's church was essentially Southern Baptist. I was taught to believe that Jesus Christ was the embodiment of God and that he died for our sins. I was also taught that I was born in sin and would burn in hell unless I joined the church and was baptized by total immersion. I further learned that to keep on the good side of God I needed to attend church every Sunday and say my prayers every night on my knees. Sometimes I cheated and didn't say them until after I was in bed, but when I did that, I felt enormous guilt. Despite my parents' diligence and years of Sunday school lessons—I've probably read the bible through a couple of times—I was not convinced that all or any of this was true.

As a very young child I recall having the idea that Jesus was human just like the rest of us, except he was good *all the time* to show us it was possible. The story of his death and resurrection—a story that has been a part of human mythology since long before the time of Jesus—symbolizes the power each of us has to rise above the calamities that are an inevitable part of life. I never questioned the existence of God, but I definitely had my doubts about his being so mean. On the one hand we were taught that God is love, but we were also told that God was wrathful and vengeful and would make us burn in hell for eternity if we crossed him. Even as a child I could see the contradiction in that. It also didn't make sense to me that people stopped being inspired to write about God once the bible was completed. I thought God must have had something he wanted us to know since that long-ago time. I decided the family church was mistaken about many things, but kept these thoughts to myself. I knew better than to openly question church doctrine. If I had said anything like this out loud, my parents would have been horrified at my blasphemy and probably would have whipped me so I would never say such things again.

Once science began to explain how natural events occur, some decided that science could be used to give humans more control. For example, they used insecticides to increase crop yields, but failed to consider that we operate within a balanced system. Insecticides not only killed crop "pests," but destroyed the bees essential for plant pollination. In many ways our society has become so enamored with technology that whatever cannot be measured or touched has been considered either nonexistent or irrelevant. Spirituality has no place in this concrete world.

For me, the discoveries of scientists, physicists in particular, have strengthened my understanding of God or Om, as Alexander refers to this energy in *Proof of Heaven*. When I learned that paying attention to particles made them move, it reinforced what I'd experienced when I focused completely on something. Whenever I've been guided to seek a specific goal, everything lines up to help me accomplish it. The same thing happens when I have a visceral fear of something—I attract it to me.

I know God/Om as interactive, not demanding; as experiences, not a person. On my best days I feel the energy of love, compassion and acceptance of everyone and everything on the planet as it currently exists, including me. I often remind myself of this statement from *The Science of Being Great* by Wallace Wattles, "THIS MUST BE YOUR POINT OF VIEW: THAT THE WORLD AND ALL IT CONTAINS IS PERFECT, THOUGH NOT COMPLETED." I am a perfect being, at the perfect point in my journey of learning and evolving; not completed yet, but moving in that direction. I believe this to be the case for each of us and for the world collectively.

At other times I am aware of Om's care when I unexpectedly receive a request for my services in time to earn the money I need for some yet unknown event. I believe that God is wherever and whoever you need God to be. If it nurtures, comforts and guides you to think of Jesus as God, to envision God as a wise old man, as Mother Nature, or to doubt the existence of any higher power, then that's a part of your journey, your evolution.

The God I believe in is an inclusive come-as-you-are God. For me God is this intelligent, dynamic, spiritual and harmoniously organized system in which we live. I also believe that each part of this system is an expression of the whole, in other words, everyone and everything is an expression of Om. When we reach the point where everybody and everything is working together according to each person's natural inclinations, that will be heaven/nirvana. However, we humans frequently push back against the natural order of things to make things happen in a way that inflates our egos. In that way we express our ability to think and exercise free will, gifts we were designed to have. We harm ourselves, the environment and each other, but the orderly, intelligent plan of the universe continues to evolve toward completion.

I am aware that not many will agree with my perception of God, but I'm not proselytizing for an institution so I don't need adherents. My relationship with God is internal. Although I welcome and enjoy validation from external sources like Deepak Chopra's *How to Know God*, that affirmation is not required. I also cherish being part of communities who share similar God experiences, but sharing is not essential to my beliefs.

Spirituality and Organized Religion

The whole point in being alive is to evolve into the complete person you were intended to be.

~ Oprah Winfrey

I AM ON A QUEST TO BECOME THE COMPLETE person I am meant to be, so my only interest in religion is when I believe it will enhance my spiritual development. I have long avoided organized religion largely because I have found little spirituality there. I often get stuck on my expectation that ministers, pastors, and spiritual leaders will be exemplars of the ethereal life they promote. What I keep learning is that religious organizations and their leaders usually have *unstated purposes* that often overshadow spiritual concerns. Most structured hierarchical religious organizations, in addition to their declared mission to "spread the gospel and save souls," have another goal to socialize members so they all believe and behave a specific way.

Other unstated aims are meant to facilitate personal ambitions within the organization (and sometimes outside as well) and to protect the institution's reputation and its traditions (often including barring women from leadership). The huge, international **Catholic Church** has shown us an example of adherence to unstated purposes in the way it handled the calamity of priests sexually molesting children. The Catholic leaders' zeal to protect the institution obliterated their ethics and overwhelmed any concern they had for the children whose healthy development was jeopardized by those priests. The survival of the organization and its reputation has obviously been more important to these leaders than the spiritual life of their congregants.

It seems to me that a rigidly structured religious hierarchy is for people who want specific guidelines for, and approval of, the way they live their lives, or a part of their lives. Some religious organizations have strict and didactic systems including dress codes, dietary restrictions, and limitations on social interactions. This type of inflexibility works best for those who prefer not to make their own decisions. I, on the other hand, *like* having choices.

The best selling book, *The Shack* by William Paul Young describes it this way. "Once you have a hierarchy you need rules to protect and administer it, and then you need law and the enforcement of the rules and you end up with some kind of chain of command or a system of order that destroys relationship rather than promotes it."

I grew up with parents who, following the tradition into which they were born, were active members of a black Baptist church. Our entire family was active in church and we attended every week. We learned that being a Christian meant loving everybody and helping those who were less fortunate. I am grateful for this upbringing because it is the base from which my spiritual explorations began. The older I got, though, the less interested I was in going to church. Our religion took all the fun out of life by classifying so many things as "sinful"—going to movies on Sunday, playing cards, dancing, enjoying life. It also seemed that being a Christian meant you were *supposed* to suffer.

In the way life often seems to mock you, after I'd been married for a couple of years, my husband shocked me one Sunday during church services by announcing that he had been called to preach. I was horrified! It was enough that I was still going to church, but I could not be the wife of a preacher. At the time I doubted his call, but even had I accepted it as authentic, I knew I had not been called to be a preacher's wife. After the marriage ended, I moved away and, for the first time, lived according to my own preferences. I stopped going to church. Initially I felt guilty about breaking the lifelong habit, but after a while I adjusted quite nicely. It was great to have a lazy day to sleep in at the end of every week; and that's what I did for the next ten years.

About a year after we moved to Boston, when my son was seven years old, I became friends with another woman, also parenting alone, who had a son about the same age. She belonged to a United Methodist Church that had a dynamic, intelligent young minister and encouraged me to join as well. I agreed, thinking that being active in a church would be helpful socially, and it was. I also thought my son's life should include the black church experience, a major component of African American culture. As it turned out, he didn't find church services any more satisfying than I did; he preferred to do "fun" things with his Sundays, like visiting a museum or going to a movie. After we moved to Chicago, we dropped church from our weekly activities.

The one thing I always liked about black churches was the passion and joy of gospel music, and Chicago was a great place to indulge that fondness. While I lived there I was lucky enough to attend the 90th birthday celebration for the legendary gospel singer and songwriter Sallie Martin. The event was held in November 1985 (I still have the program) at Fellowship Baptist Church, pastored by the Reverend Clay Evans, a gospel singer of some note himself. It was like a one-night gospel festival and I enjoyed it immensely. On occasional Sundays, I'd visit a church known for its great choir and get my fill for a few months until I wanted another "fix." Unfortunately, I wasn't bold enough to leave before the preaching began, so after sitting through too many bombastic sermons, not even a fabulous choir could lure me into a church.

The one place I could count on both great music and a provocative sermon was Trinity United Church of Christ, where Jeremiah Wright was the senior pastor. Even Wright's black liberation theology, however, was not enough to keep me coming on a regular basis. After a while, Chicago inaugurated an annual Gospel Festival along with their Blues and Jazz festivals. There I could get my fill of gospel music without sitting through a sermon. Problem solved.

It was in Chicago that I began to work earnestly on becoming a better person and better parent. This led me to psychotherapy and to an interest in books on metaphysics and spirituality. What I read dispelled much of what I'd been taught. I saw *in print* the secret, sacrilegious thoughts I'd had since I was a child, such as the idea that not only Jesus, but all humans are expressions of God. My reading confirmed the notion I had that people continue to receive inspiration from God/the Universe/the Source/Allah just as they did in the past.

Some of the reading also reinforced messages in familiar biblical passages, like the Twenty-third Psalm—"Though I walk through the valley of the shadow of death, I will fear no evil..."—and the tenth verse of Psalm 46—"Be still and know that I am God." And my favorite, chapter four, eighth verse of Philippians—"Finally, brethren, whatsoever things are true, whatsoever things are honest, whatsoever things are just, whatsoever things are pure, whatsoever things are lovely, whatsoever things are of good report; if there be any virtue, and if there be any praise, think on these things." Reading these books, along with gaining insights from my therapy sessions, supported my spiritual growth and helped me to understand and appreciate myself and my world more than anything I'd encountered in decades of attending church.

For over twenty years, I attended church only for weddings and funerals and that felt fine to me. I continued my study of metaphysical and spiritual texts and found them thoroughly satisfying. Then unexpectedly, a dear friend died while I was on an extended writing retreat. I wanted additional support in grieving her death and asked to attend service with friends at a Spiritual

Center. I expected that a spiritual center would be less authoritarian than the churches I had attended, and I was right. The service was similar to that of a church, but less formal, including lay leadership and inclusive language, most of which corresponded with the spiritual principles I had come to accept, including that Jesus was an extraordinary human, not a god to be worshipped. The music didn't match the fervor of gospel singing, but the lyrics were inspiring and supportive of my spiritual quest. The best part was the several minutes of meditation which prepared us for the service. I loved that! I also joined a group that spent an hour before the service reading and discussing empowering books and learned much that contributed to my spiritual growth. My satisfaction with this Center waned as new structures were instituted. More emphasis was placed on ties to the national organization, and services felt more doctrinaire than inspirational.

I've come to understand that people who have been "ordained" as ministers/spiritual leaders are, like the rest of us, on a spiritual journey. I may wish they were more spiritually evolved than the people they "lead," and some no doubt are, but I should not *expect* that to be the case. Each person is evolving into the complete person they are intended to be, no matter what field they're in. For me it's writing, for some it's entertaining, for others parenting, teaching, healing, seeking justice, running a business. In every field there are people who have evolved to a high spiritual level, others who are in the early stages of opening to spiritual guidance and some who are not yet aware of their spiritual potential. It is not mine to suppose where anyone should be on that journey. However, I will choose the company I keep.

Link:

Catholic Church http://www.nytimes.com/2012/09/11/opinion/bruni-suffer-the-children.html?_r=0

Using My Consciousness

Most people live, whether physically, intellectually or morally, in a very restricted circle of their potential being. They make use of a very small portion of their possible consciousness.

~ **William James**

I LAVISHED MY ONLY CHILD WITH THE AFFECTION and verbal expressions of love I had longed for while I was growing up. My siblings and I knew our parents loved us because they took good care of us and did lots of fun things with us, but they did not say so and they were not affectionate. My son and I, however, were and are spontaneous and generous in expressions of love. The love of my child and my desire to be the best possible parent made me want to become a better person. I began with psychotherapy, and that was helpful, but more important was my exploration of spiritual and metaphysical matters.

My interest in spirituality was initiated by a chapter from *Living in the Light* by Shakti Gawain that I read in a magazine. In the excerpted chapter, Gawain wrote about the power of intuition. For the first time I realized that those premonitory feelings I had always pushed aside, meant something. That revelation reinforced a saying I'd heard many times: "Always listen to your first mind." I bought a copy of Gawain's book and was mesmerized by it. In it I read support for many of my private beliefs. Throughout my life I have received knowledge/information that didn't come from anyplace specific, I just *knew*. For many years I thought everybody received information this way, but slowly discovered that was not the case. (Or, perhaps they did, but didn't pay attention.) I started looking for and reading more books like Gawain's.

I read Wayne Dyer's *The Sky's the Limit*, in which he encourages people not to limit themselves; and Deepak Chopra's *Seven Spiritual Laws of Success*, an introductory look at spiritual laws that affect all of life. While I was reading these books, *The Oprah Winfrey Show* spent a year on spiritual matters, and I watched as often as I could. Gary Zukav was one of Oprah's guests and I read his book, *Seat of the Soul*. Zukav's book helped me to see an aspect of my character that was blocking my continued growth. I later read *The Dark Side of the Light Chasers* by Debbie Ford and it furthered my understanding that it is necessary to see myself holistically—to accept the light and the dark side of who I am. In addition I spent hours watching PBS specials featuring inspirational speakers like Les Brown, Christiane Northrup, Dyer and Chopra. Reading these books, repeatedly watching the videos, and undergoing five years of psychotherapy helped me to understand myself far better than I ever thought possible and to gradually remove what I thought of as a protective shell around my heart.

This brief description is provided as background for an extraordinary experience I had. In 2008, my older brother James told the family he was ill and would not live much longer. He had been diagnosed with cancer a few years earlier and chose not to have it treated. He said he'd lived long enough and done everything he wanted to do. I was hurt and saddened to learn he was near death, but not completely surprised because he had been looking increasingly frail, though he insisted he was in good health. Once I knew he was nearing the end of his life, whenever I visited I made a point of hugging him long and closely and saying, "I love you." Although I'd long since started to hug friends and family, I believe it was the first time I'd ever told my brother I loved him. He didn't return my hugs (perhaps he was too weak) or respond in any physical way, but I could feel his gratitude. A couple of months after he admitted he was ill, he died at age seventy-five, at home as he preferred.

For many years I've kept journals in which I write how I feel about the events of my life and record the lessons I learn. I also write down what I remember of my dreams from the night before. Writing out the dreams helps me interpret the symbols they usually contain. In 2009 I read *The Power of Premonitions* by Larry Dossey, in which he wrote about the number of people who'd had premonitions about September 11, 2001. I decided to check my journal for that year to see if I'd had a premonition about that fateful day. I had not. However, as I looked through the journal I was surprised to find these words written on October 18, 2001: "Last night I dreamed that I saw James, my older brother. He looked young, but very sick. I knew he was dying and so did he. I gave him a hug because I knew he was longing for love. I pray that his life is peaceful and contented."

Many times I've heard or read that linear time is perceptual and does not exist, that in reality everything is happening all at once. I've thought about this concept, but it remains beyond my grasp; however, when I (or anyone) see into the "future" like this, is it because Spiritual Intelligence is revealing something I need to know, or is it just a random glimpse of something else that is going on at the same time? One definition of premonition is "a warning." But my brother died *seven years* after I had the dream! By then I no longer remembered the "warning." Or, did I? Perhaps the memory of that dream was lodged in my subconscious encouraging me to express my love for him.

The presentiment about my brother was startling because it was so precise. I've had other dreams with a message about a future occurrence, but they are usually not literal. For example, I dreamed I saw a dear friend dead in a casket. The dream was so vivid and I was so disturbed by it that I called her the next day to make sure she was alive and well. Two months later that friend called to tell me she had been diagnosed with separate cancers in each breast. There's no way I would have told my friend I saw her dead in a dream, so the "warning" was apparently meant to prepare me to receive her news. I do recall one dream warning that was immediately useful. I was sound asleep and dreamed my then four-year-old son was hanging head-first over the edge of a cliff. The terrifying image woke me up. I got out of bed and went across the hall to check on him. I found him on his back hanging over the side of his bed, head first. I lifted him back up on his bed, tucked him in and put a chair there to block him from sliding into that position again.

Not only have I pondered where these dreams come from, but I also wonder what effect they have on me. Does having information ahead of the actual event in any way alter my perception of the event when it occurs, even when I have no conscious memory of the dream?

I also have premonitions when I'm awake, but these are called intuition, and I ignore them at my peril. When I make plans to do something and there's a sense of looming disaster in my body, I should not carry through with the plans. Initially, I mistook this foreboding as a silly fear of trying something new and dismissed it while I plowed ahead. One of the great things about experience, however, is that I can look back and review what happened when I disregarded that feeling. It has taken repeated failures, but now I know the difference between foreboding and fear of risk-taking. Although I cannot adequately describe the feelings, they are emphatically different! I had a palpable sense of dread when I decided to move my business out of my home to an office in downtown Chicago. The move turned out to be a huge money-eating mistake that nearly crushed a thriving business.

On the other hand, an earlier flash of intuition that it was time to leave my corporate job and do something on my own was sound. As soon as I had the thought I *knew* it was exactly what I needed to do. I also knew I would move to Chicago because I'd always wanted to live there. Immediately, the world moved to assist me, in often surprising ways. Soon after I had those insights, my employer asked me to go to Chicago on business. When I put my home on the market, I received an offer from the first person who looked at it. In Chicago things continued to fall effortlessly into place. I clearly remember adding my gross receipts at the end of my third year and observing the geometric growth. Instead of being buoyed by that information, I became alarmed that my good fortune wouldn't continue and a whole new phase of my life began.

I understand and accept my gut-level indicator of which actions to pursue and which to avoid. I trust my precognition and believe my premonitions, intuition, and dreams are evidence that I am part of an encompassing Intelligence beyond myself.

Immortality: Beyond Marble or Monuments

Not marble, nor the gilded monuments
Of princes, shall outlive this powerful rhyme;
But you shall shine more bright in these contents
Than unswept stone, besmear'd with sluttish time.
When wasteful war shall statues overturn,
And broils root out the work of masonry,
Nor Mars his sword, nor war's quick fire shall burn
The living record of your memory.

~ **William Shakespeare, from Sonnet 55**

THE PRACTICE OF NAMING PUBLIC and university edifices for persons deemed to have given extraordinary service is rapidly giving way to commercial labeling. Some people with material wealth donate millions of dollars to universities, thereby allowing (encouraging, mandating?) the university to name a building for them, "guaranteeing" their immortality. It is a way for universities to obtain money, and I doubt they question the motives of the donor. Everything has its purpose in this orderly universe.

No matter how large or sturdy the building, however, immortality cannot be guaranteed or purchased. Most folk outside the local community have no idea how or why a person's name came to be on a building. Even some locals don't know why an institution has a particular name. I recall the flap that occurred when a Midwestern university decided to change the name of an athletic stadium named for a revered coach. The coach's name had been on the stadium for many years. Although contemporary students knew nothing of him, nostalgic alumni and the family of the discarded coach were publicly unhappy about the removal of his familiar name. The university, however, had decided to sell the naming rights to a corporation. The income they'd receive was worth more than any sentiment about tradition. Such is the "immortality"of gilded monuments.

The actual immortals, those people who are influential, referenced, and quoted, and whose names have been venerated over time are usually those who were not seeking immortality, but rather surrendering to the spirit of adding beauty and value to the world. Interestingly, many of these people during their lifetimes were not honored, but vilified or even killed. I am referring to people like Susan B. Anthony, John Brown, Galileo Galilei, Mohandas Gandhi, Zora Neale Hurston, Jesus, Martin Luther King Jr., Jeannette Rankin, Socrates, Harriet Tubman, Lao Tzu and Oscar Wilde.

What is awarded and praised in a particular time and place may lose value when seen from the distance of many years. The posthumous recognition of people like those listed above lends credence to Kahlil Gibran's statement, "You give but little when you give of your possessions. It is when you give of yourself that you truly give." These people gave of themselves, even when they were denounced and abused for their efforts. However, over time humanity has come to appreciate the significance of their contributions and the courage required of them to pursue their beliefs. Examples like these encourage me to focus on what feels right to me and what feeds my soul rather than what may currently be popular.

Using
Communal Power

The Big White Lie:
America's Racial Paradigm

*The pervasive violence in our society—from domestic abuse
to economic exploitation to capital punishment to punitive
expeditionary wars—is rooted in the paradigm of race.*

~ John Edgar Wideman in *Fatheralong*

WHITE SUPREMACISTS SHOULD BE ANXIOUS and distressed.
The story they've perpetrated for centuries about their superiority over women, "people of color," and gays is unraveling right
before their eyes. Not only is there an African American President of the United States, but there is only one "straight" white
male in the **top ten** of *Forbes* 2014 list of highest-earning celebrities. And fully half of the entire list are people from the groups
traditionally marginalized by white supremacists. It's enough to
make them all quake in their boots.

I've been exposed to America's racial paradigm for three-
quarters of a century; what I write here is based on what I've
lived and what I've learned from reading history in works other
than official classroom texts. As the PBS documentary ***Race:
The Power of an Illusion*** explains, "Race has no genetic basis."
Instead, it "is a powerful social idea that gives people different
access to opportunities and resources." However, scientific data
means nothing in the presence of this powerful social imperative.

The murders of Oscar Grant (January 1, 2009) in Oakland,
California and Trayvon Martin (February 26, 2012) in Sanford,
Florida are but two high-profile examples of how racism permeates American society. I have grieved along with the parents of
both young men, although certainly not as deeply, over these
easily avoidable calamities. The grief feels personal because it

rekindles the fear that I, and most parents of black male children, live with daily. We know that at any moment some person (police officer, random gun-toter) could see your child's black maleness as a threat that has to be eradicated. And numerous precedents have taught these would-be "guardians" they will not be punished for these murders.

After considerable delay, Trayvon Martin's confessed killer was finally taken into custody and charged with second-degree murder. However, for six weeks he was at liberty to kill again while some media diligently sought to tarnish the character of the victim. The media assault on the victim was led by the town of Sanford's law enforcement. Although police took the murderer into custody for possible detention, they were overruled by higher authorities and told to let him go. These same authorities tested Trayvon Martin's dead body for drugs, but didn't test or even question the murderer, whose "reason" for stalking and killing an innocent, unarmed youth was that he acted in self-defense.

Oscar Grant was killed by an officer of the law while lying handcuffed, face down on the ground. The officer "mistakenly" used his gun when he "meant" to use a taser. Why would either weapon have been necessary when the subject is prone on the ground and handcuffed behind his back?

The white men who committed these murders are both free to murder again. Trayvon's murderer was found not guilty of any charges and the officer who killed Grant, although found guilty of *involuntary* manslaughter, served eleven months of a two-year sentence. These two cases remind us yet again that some things haven't changed in the last 150 years. In 1857 the U.S. Supreme Court ruled in **Dred Scott *v.* Sanford** that blacks "had no rights which the white man was bound to respect . . . ."

It has been dismaying, although not surprising, to see racism's ugly head spinning wildly after Barack Obama was elected President of the United States. Having our first black president seems to have unhinged a sizable number of Americans, most visibly those in the Tea/Republican Party, but thankfully they are not the majority. These tea partiers are outraged at having a black man in the White House and, in addition to insulting the president in every possible way they can think of, they are passing and pushing for laws to take us back in time, to their "glory" days. Apparently they're longing for the days when people with "a drop of African blood" couldn't vote, let alone run for president. To achieve that end they are erecting new barriers to the right to vote, especially for black and brown folks. This is step one back to the days they long for when only propertied white males were allowed to vote.

For these disturbed Americans, President Obama's election has concretized the warning that Patrick Buchanan has been issuing for years, most specifically in his book, *State of Emergency: The Third World Invasion and Conquest of America*. "Third world" is his euphemism for people who are not white. That title, and the mythology of a white America that so many want to return to, represent the Big White Lie.

THIS HAS NEVER BEEN A WHITE COUNTRY

The only "invasion" of America has been by whites—people who looked like Buchanan. This has never been a white country. There were no whites (i.e., Europeans) here when the first immigrants made contact with the people already living on this land. These immigrant Europeans utilized their more efficient weaponry to invade and occupy the land, systematically displacing or killing the indigenous people. They succeeded in taking control, but the original inhabitants they dubbed "Indians" survive and continue to have a presence, however marginal, in their ancestral homeland.

Europeans had been engaged in the **capture and sale of Africans** for more than a century when they "discovered" the New World. So it was a no-brainer in 1619 to bring Africans across the Atlantic to do the back-breaking work of developing the new country and making the most of the land's resources. Europeans held the reins of power, but the country was not "white" because the original inhabitants were still present, and the number of Africans was rapidly increasing, especially in the South, where much of the slave labor was concentrated. In what was to become the United States, immigrants from Europe gradually set aside their disdain for each other—muting regional prejudices and national differences—to become "white" and thereby establish a cohesive group superiority over the "nonwhites" in their midst. The population of "colored" people expanded exponentially as white males took advantage of their power to rape the "inferior" women. The offspring of these *legitimate* rapes further diluted the number of whites.

In 1848 the Treaty of Guadalupe Hidalgo placed a significant portion of Mexico (including what are now the states of California, Nevada, Utah, Arizona, New Mexico, and part of Colorado and Texas) and *Mexicans* within the United States, increasing the number of "colored" citizens in America yet again. The suffusion continued with the importation of Chinese laborers to build the Transcontinental Railroad completed in 1869. The U.S. acquired Puerto Rico (there are more Puerto Ricans in this country than in Puerto Rico) the Philippines, and Guam after defeating Spain in the 1898 Spanish-American War. American imperialism brought along other "nonwhite territories" like Samoa, the Virgin Islands, Alaska and Hawaii, the latter two admitted as the 49th and 50th states in 1959. The "nonwhite" people living in these territories are all Americans. U. S. military incursions in Southeast Asia and the Middle East have spurred refugees and immigrants from these non-European areas to settle here. The term "nonwhite" is itself the perfect indicator of the assumed supremacy of whiteness.

Now that the national stew is nicely spiced and these people of color are exercising their power, a number of whites are hysterically digging in their heels in a desire to "take their country back." Fear of becoming a "minority" in "their" country is what built the fence on the Mexican border, toughened immigration restrictions, and increased deportations. Their rage for more prisons had long been fueled by a desire to re-enslave blacks—African and Hispanic Americans make up approximately 25 percent of the nation's population, yet they constitute *more than half* of those incarcerated in the country's prisons. Now, however, the hungry and rapacious privatized prison industry is gobbling up poor whites as well. (In 1998 an *Atlantic* article stated, "The United States now **imprisons more people** than any other country in the world— perhaps half a million more than Communist China." And the **numbers have increased** since that article was written.)

What these frightened folk don't realize is that their hysteria is much too late. Dragging their heels will only create deep ruts. It's inevitable, people of color will be the majority, and soon. Not because of any "invasion" as Buchanan and others want us to believe. Rather, this demographic shift is a result of long-standing official U.S. policies and imperialist practices that crafted a racial paradigm in the United States dating back to the first European immigrants.

I agree with award-winning writer **John Edgar Wideman's** description of a racial paradigm as "a vision of humankind and society based on the premise that not all people are created equal and some are born with the right to exploit others."

With the media's constant barrage of statistics, African Americans are not allowed to forget that we are regarded as not measuring up to the white standard. That makes it easier for officials and others to see African Americans as disposable. For many years we were *the* defective ethnic group, but as their numbers increase, Hispanic Americans have been added to the mix. Since 2001, people from the Middle East, or those who look like they could be from that area, have been added to the list of suspects. On occasion it may be mentioned, in passing, that even whites are surpassed in achievement by the "model" ethnic group—Asian Americans. Note that all measurements are taken by *race/ethnic group,* not by levels of wealth, achievement or education, but by ethnic group. Why? Because America operates in a racial paradigm.

What is never mentioned, or hardly even alluded to, is that despite their status as the standard to which everyone else is compared, some whites *feel the full measure of their inadequacies* until reminded that *at least they are not black/Hispanic/foreign,* at which time they can swell with pride. My guess is that the only time George Zimmerman felt powerful and sure of himself was when he and his gun were circling the neighborhood looking for "suspicious/black" persons.

In an insightful article that sets Trayvon's murder within American history, **Melissa Harris-Perry,** writing for *The Nation,* provides a succinct response to the claim that racism was not involved. "Trayvon Martin was not innocent. He was guilty of being black in presumably restricted public space. For decades, Jim Crow laws made this crime statutory." **Don Washington** in his article "Permission Granted" argues convincingly that society has given permission for the murders/attempted murders of Trayvon, Brandon Teena, Gabby Giffords and many others. Permission was granted, he says, "To enforce the natural order of things as ordained by God, informed and encouraged by legitimate media and political leaders and written into law by society itself." It's the violence Wideman cites as being "rooted in the paradigm of race" spreading to high school bullies, spreading to the mentally unstable, spreading, spreading, spreading . . . .

Harris-Perry, Washington and Wideman are referring to the systemic racism in America that permeates our government, our media, and our economic, political, social, educational, legal, and religious institutions. Racism is integral to who Americans are, to what the U. S. has been since its inception and still is. Yet we refuse to face it, or even acknowledge its existence. Instead, government officials, political leaders, the media, pundits and others continue to invoke the Big White Lie. We are caught like a bug in a spider's web—the more we thrash about, the tighter the web becomes because we refuse to recognize what's gripping us.

Links:

top ten http://www.forbes.com/celebrities/

Race: The Power of an Illusion http://newsreel.org/video/RACE-THE-POWER-OF-AN-ILLUSION

Dred Scott v. Sanford http://www.pbs.org/wgbh/aia/part4/4h2933.html

capture and sale of Africans http://honoringtheheart.com/
Through the Lens of the African Slave Trade by Vinita Moch Ricks, Ph.D.

more than half http://www.naacp.org/pages/criminal-justice-fact-sheet

imprisons more people http://www.theatlantic.com/magazine/archive/1998/12/the-prison-industrial-complex/304669/

numbers have increased http://content.time.com/time/magazine/article/0,9171,2109777,00.html

John Edgar Wideman http://brown.edu/Departments/Africana_Studies/people/wideman_john.html

Melissa Harris-Perry http://www.thenation.com/article/167085/trayvon-martin-what-its-be-problem

Don Washington http://mayoraltutorial.com/articles/permission_granted

The Viewer's Involvement

The work itself has a complete circle of meaning and counterpoint.... And without your involvement as a viewer, there is no story.

~ Anish Kapoor

WHEN I WAS VISITING CHICAGO my friend Lucille Freeman asked me to join her to see the movie *Precious*. I had heard about the movie and seen previews, so I didn't expect it to be either entertaining or informative, and it wasn't. Lucille, whose expectations were higher than mine, was acutely disappointed with everything about the movie. I was impressed with Gabourey Sidibe's performance, which was exceptional, especially for a novice actor, but Lucille was in no mood to grant even that. As more people saw the movie, I read and heard that many of them—especially whites—loved it and were moved and inspired by it. I was startled. What did they see that we didn't?

Barbara Bush, a wealthy woman of European descent, wife of one U.S. president and mother of another, invited two hundred of her friends over for a screening of *Precious*. **Mrs. Bush was quoted** as saying, "The movie is so strong and so honest." Mrs. Bush's admiration and my own revulsion have everything to do with our different experiences in this country.

My perception of the movie cannot be separated from seventy-plus years of being on the receiving end of countless racist experiences, both personal and institutional. One of those experiences has been watching the film industry and other media insidiously manipulate the images and angles through which African Americans are viewed. This manipulation has been going on so long and been so consistent and pervasive I could write a book about it, but Donald Bogle already did: *Toms, Coons, Mulattoes, Mammies and Bucks: An Interpretive History of Blacks in American Films.* This popular book was originally published in 1973 and is currently in its fourth edition, updated to include the entire twentieth century. Mr. Bogle will need more updates as the pattern continues into the twenty-first century.

I didn't need to see a movie like *Precious* to know that some people live awful, brutal lives; I've met people coping with similar lives, both white and black. Early on I thought the movie meant to show a possible way out for those who are struggling in such situations. However, at the end of the movie, Precious is single, unemployed, HIV-positive, and homeless with two children, one of whom has Down Syndrome. I saw no indication of how she would extricate herself from this dire situation. The movie felt punitive because I paid good money to spend nearly two hours watching somebody's worst nightmare unfold. And for what purpose, or to what end? Was this a voyeuristic pleasure for somebody? What young woman in anything approximating those conditions would be helped or inspired by this movie? Precious's signal achievement, the one that apparently made such an impression on Barbara Bush, is that she learns to read. Reading can certainly be empowering; however, I know folks who read quite well and are still incapacitated by our winner-take-all society.

It did not surprise me that Academy Award nominations were rained on *Precious;* it's in keeping with the Academy's history of honoring particular types of roles played by black actors. Among the more than 300 Oscars handed out since 1927, fewer than twenty have gone to black people. The winning roles for black actors have largely been when they played characters that conform to conventional white expectations for African Americans—servants, slaves, musicians/athletes, or people who were corrupt and/or cruel. The black actors who have received Academy Awards for both leading or supporting roles are: Hattie McDaniel (a maid in *Gone With the Wind,* 1940), Sidney Poitier (a handyman in *Lilies of the Field,* 1964), Denzel Washington (a slave in *Glory,* 1990), Whoopi Goldberg (a dishonest psychic in *Ghost,* 1991), Cuba Gooding Jr. (a boxer in *Jerry Maguire,* 1997) Halle Berry (a waitress in *Monster's Ball,* 2002), Jamie Foxx (the singer Ray Charles in *Ray,* 2005), Morgan Freeman (a former boxer in *Million Dollar Baby,* 2005), Jennifer Hudson (a singer in *Dreamgirls,* 2007) and Mo'Nique (a brutal and abusive mother in *Precious,* 2010).

In 2012, the Academy returned to where it began with Mc-Daniel, awarding an Oscar to Octavia Spencer for her role as a maid in *The Help.* In 2013 two movies about American slavery—*Lincoln* and *Django Unchained*— received lots of attention. Both included black actors; however neither of the award winners for these movies was black. (Jamie Foxx was not the right kind of slave.) There was another slave movie released in time to be considered for the 2014 awards. That movie excited the country so much, they totally forgot about the movie they were marveling about earlier in the year. In my opinion, and I wasn't alone in this, *Fruitvale Station* was an excellent movie that dealt directly with contemporary issues. And that, no doubt, was its undoing. Why focus on a movie that makes people squirm when you have a perfectly good movie set in the distant past that reassures us all that we've made so much progress. *Twelve Years a Slave* wowed movie goers and received the 2014 Best Picture award. The black director, Steve McQueen, apparently was not so impressive. He managed to direct the Best Picture, but he was not the Best Director. Lupita Nyong'o was superb and received an award for Best Supporting Actor in her role as, *surprise!* a slave.

The dubious exceptions that prove this insidious rule are Louis Gossett (*An Officer and a Gentleman,* 1983) and Forest Whitaker (*The Last King of Scotland,* 2007), who won Oscars as strong military men, though both characters were stern and pitiless. In the same year *Precious* was released, Morgan Freeman starred in *Invictus* as Nelson Mandela, one of the most inspirational figures of our time. Although Freeman was nominated, I was certain that a role depicting a black man as a shrewd, resourceful, inspiring leader would not receive an Oscar. I was right.

By celebrating only roles that are subservient, cruel, demeaning and/or within an "acceptable" profession, Hollywood's majority reinforces America's assumption of white dominance. The case of Denzel Washington is a stark illustration of this practice. Washington is one of the most talented actors ever; he *became* Malcolm X and Rubin "Hurricane" Carter in the title roles of two films about complex and *empowered* black men—*Malcolm X* (1992) and *Hurricane* (1999). The Academy Award voters didn't find either of those to be winning performances. In 2002 when Washington finally received an Oscar as best actor in a *leading* role, it was for *Training Day*, a film in which he played a brutal and crooked cop who gets blasted to bits. That was a role he could be honored for.

So far as I'm concerned, Hollywood has a long, long, loooong way to go to make up for the Denzel Washington travesty. And they have yet to take a step on that road. In 2015 there were critically acclaimed and successful movies starring black actors, yet not one black actor was nominated for an award.

I learned that **Academy voters** for Oscar winners are 94% white and 74% male, average age 63. Until the make-up of Academy voters becomes more representative of the country, the biases will continue.

Links:

Mrs. Bush was quoted
   http://www.npr.org/templates/story/story.php?storyId=121335962

Academy voters
   http://www.theatlantic.com/entertainment/archive/2014/03/oscar-voters-94-white-76-men-and-an-average-of-63-years-old/284163/

The Help: How to Comfort Whites

(adapted from a blog originally published online by *San Francisco Weekly*)

If you look for truth, you may find comfort in the end:
if you look for comfort, you will not get either comfort or
truth—only soft soap and wishful thinking to begin with,
and in the end, despair.

~ **C.S. Lewis**

I WASN'T MUCH INTERESTED IN *The Help* by Kathryn Stockett until the book became all the rage and was made into a movie. The book was a quick read that I enjoyed largely because I was surprised that a woman who *hired* help, rather than *being* "the help," seemed to capture that mixture of devotion and disgust that people have when they clean up after their "betters." I am familiar with that feeling because I've been a maid. Your devotion is to doing a good job, your disgust is that they believe your only value lies in your doing their bidding.

I assume *The Help* is autobiographical, set in the past so Stockett's Mississippi family and friends wouldn't be offended. Otherwise I can't fathom how anybody could write a book about blacks in Mississippi in the 1960s and virtually ignore the civil rights upheavals. Obviously, it was not part of the author's consciousness or important to the story she wanted to tell. My experience has been that white families (the traditional employers of "help,") usually don't have a clue how their black maids feel about them, so because Stockett got some of it right, it's clear to me that she listened to some maids, or *a maid*. **Ablene Cooper**, her brother's maid, sued Stockett because she believes the character, Aibileen Clark, "is an unauthorized appropriation of [Cooper's] name and image." Of course Stockett has to insist it's a work of fiction. The **lawsuit was dismissed** because it was filed after the statute of limitations had passed.

Stockett wrote the story she wanted to write and I have no issue with that. What bothers me is yet another example of the black-people-don't-exist-until-white-people-notice syndrome. Black women (including me) have written books about being maids and nobody cared. When a white person writes about black life, their books become best sellers, the media takes note, and the movie studios get out their checkbooks. It's *Black Like Me* all over again.

I understand why *The Help* struck a huge responsive chord in America and was so quickly made into a movie. In what is allegedly post-racial America, whites can read the book, watch the movie and congratulate themselves because they never were, or no longer are, as racist as those women. *The Help* is proof that, indeed, "that kind of thing" is history. The other, more subtle message that is oddly (and likely unconsciously) comforting, is being reminded of the place the majority of black folk have occupied for most of our American experience. This nostalgia mitigates the unsettling idea of an African American as U.S. president, a fact that has rattled the poise of a number of people. Undoubtedly there is concern in some quarters that black folks could get the big head and start thinking they are equal to whites. The first movie about blacks that was wildly popular after President Obama's election was *Precious;* a film depicting a brutally dysfunctional black family so no one would be fooled by the one in the White House. What a hit it was! And it's popularity was acknowledged by SIX Academy Award nominations!

I am not suggesting a conspiracy. It isn't necessary for a group to sit down and decide that *The Help* should become a bestseller and be dramatized in a movie. The image of faithful black servants is as American as mom, apple pie and the flag. Black folk were held as slaves four times longer than we've been "free." And for at least the first hundred years after slavery, most blacks were employed in jobs serving whites. In *Sister Citizen: Shame, Stereotypes, and Black Women in America*, Melissa Harris-Perry writes about a monument to mammies that was touted for the nation's capital in 1923. A U.S. senator proposed a bill in Congress to build a national Mammy Monument. The bill was passed by the Senate, shortly after they had defeated an anti-lynching bill. Fortunately, it did not pass the House. Harris-Perry says, "Although Mammy was never carved in granite, she was enshrined in the American imagination throughout the first half of the twentieth century."

There remains a nostalgic longing for the faithful black servant; it's the most familiar and comforting image white Americans have of blacks. That's why **Aunt Jemima** and Uncle Ben were created to market food products. As African Americans press onward in a quest for full citizenship, this vision of the "good old days" when blacks were servants is periodically resurrected as a palliative. Prior to *The Help*, we had *Driving Miss Daisy*, a 1988 Pulitzer prize winner for drama, a movie in 1989, and seemingly endless theatrical revivals since then; the *Beulah* television series, 1950-53; *Song of the South*, 1946, and the most beloved of all, *Gone With the Wind*, 1939; now available on Blu-Ray, high definition-DVD. This has been going on for a long time.

Reality television has made its own contribution to the codification of blacks as servants. One of the first "unscripted" television shows to feature African Americans was *Flavor of Love* in 2006. In *Reality Bites Back: The Troubling Truth About Guilty Pleasure TV*, Jennifer Pozner writes, "On The Bachelor, white women get to play Cinderella. On *Flavor of Love*, Black women get to play maids." In order to impress Flavor Flav, a former rapper with the group Public Enemy, and win the competition for his "love," the women had to clean his disgustingly filthy mansion. The twist in this scenario is that these women were playing maid to a black man, rather than to whites, but that hardly makes it acceptable. Pozner's book examines in detail how reality television's stock-in-trade is degrading women.

Aside from the reassurance it apparently provides, I see no reason to become excited about another book/movie showing blacks serving whites. Two years after *The Help* was published, it was on film. As the 2012 presidential campaign revved up, *The Help* was nominated for four Academy Awards and Octavia Spencer, who played one of the maids, won an Oscar for best supporting actor. So while Barack Obama was seeking re-election, the media was discussing the satisfying image of black servants, again. Ah! So comforting it almost makes up for having a black man in the White House.

Links:

Ablene Cooper http://artsbeat.blogs.nytimes.com/2011/02/17/family-maid-files-suit-against-author-of-the-help/

lawsuit was dismissed http://www.washingtonpost.com/blogs/celebritology/post/the-help-lawsuit-against-kathryn-stockett-dismissed/2011/08/16/gIQAiCWqJJ_blog.html

Black Like Me http://en.wikipedia.org/wiki/Black_Like_Me

Precious http://www.nytimes.com/2009/10/25/magazine/25precious-t.html?pagewanted=all

Aunt Jemima http://amst312.umwblogs.org/2009/02/26/aunt-jemima-pancake-flour/

Living History: Movies About Slavery

The plain truth is that slavery was an unprecedented economic juggernaut whose impact is still lived by each of us daily.

~ Imara Jones

DJANGO UNCHAINED **GENERATED A LOT** of controversy. There was angry talk about the number of times "nigger" was used—somebody counted and said it was more than a hundred. Spike Lee wouldn't see it because he said it would offend his ancestors. Others were outraged that Broomhilda (Kerry Washington's character) was a "helpless female" needing rescue. (If she had been the proverbial "strong black woman" fighting to get her husband back, we wouldn't like that either.)

When I was a child, my mother told me the only reason my brother kept calling me names was that he enjoyed getting a rise out of me. "If you ignore him," she said, "he'll stop." She was right. So I learned it's what I answer to that matters more than what you call me. Apparently, Quentin Tarantino is obsessed with the word "nigger;" but that doesn't mean we have to have the same fixation.

I thought *Django Unchained* was fun and funny. When I heard the contemporary music playing, I knew it was not a serious movie, so I relaxed. I've seen a couple of Tarantino movies and I was far more disturbed by the prospect of his signature gratuitous violence than I was about how many times "nigger" would be uttered.

Django Unchained is an ironic spoof of slavery. *Beloved* (1998) was a serious film treatment of slavery and hardly anyone saw it. Tarantino knows what puts butts in the seats: lots of big blasting guns, explosions, blood flowing freely, a damsel in distress, an invincible hero who has close calls, but will triumph in the end, and tongue-in-cheek anachronisms all over the place. In other words, Tarantino made a typical Hollywood adventure film. What is atypical is that it's set within slavery and the last man standing is black. It became **Tarantino's highest grossing film** ever.

Yes, Tarantino mocked the travesty that was slavery, but he also showed the cruelty and absurdity of it. I much prefer that to having slavery denied or lied about. And there were moments of hilarity. The night riders who couldn't see through their ineptly made hoods were a scream. The sadistic slaver who "owned" Broomhilda called his plantation "Candyland" —a silly parody of the pastoral names given to the estates of traders in human flesh. I howled to see that after all the whites were dead, Samuel Jackson's character dropped his cane, straightened his back and stopped acting servile. I also laughed when Tarantino's own character wound up as a hole in the ground, victim of one of the explosions. *Django Unchained* is cathartic, extremely violent escapism. That's why it's ridiculous that Tarantino explained his abundant use of "nigger" in this spoof as the way it was in antebellum Mississippi. My son called him on it in **this hilarious episode** of *Totally Biased with W. Kamau Bell.*

The films *Lincoln* and *12 Years a Slave,* on the other hand, are serious and can be faulted for ignoring important aspects of history pertinent to the stories. I believe *Lincoln* has resonated with so many, as it did with me, because nearly 150 years ago the U.S. Congress was as sharply polarized as it is today, and along nearly the same lines. This movie is for those who love the gamesmanship of politics. Unfortunately, by focusing solely on the white male elected officials who finally managed to make traffic in human lives illegal in the United States, Steven Spielberg has denied the monumental efforts of the many others who *forced* this political battle. This is particularly jarring because those whom

Spielberg ignores, not even giving them the courtesy of a line of dialogue, are the same ones who are historically marginalized in this society. In *Lincoln*, agency and power, as usual, is depicted as the sole province of white males.

The people totally ignored by *Lincoln* are Quakers who began resisting slavery in the seventeenth century, abolitionists who labored for decades to change public opinion from acceptance of slavery to abhorrence for it, women, and those who had been enslaved. One of the most eloquent abolitionists, the former slave, Frederick Douglass, met with President Lincoln to convince him to allow blacks to fight in the Union Army. **Eric Foner**, professor of history at Columbia University, tells us, "The 13th Amendment originated not with Lincoln but with a petition campaign early in 1864 organized by the Women's National Loyal League, an organization of abolitionist feminists headed by Susan B. Anthony and Elizabeth Cady Stanton."

To not even mention the Quakers, Douglass or the Women's National Loyal League is inexcusable.

I have less to say about *12 Years a Slave* which received critical acclaim and the 2014 Academy Award for Best Picture. I believe Academy voters were smugly applauding themselves because those gruesome days are so far behind us. They did not have the courage to even nominate the also critically-acclaimed *Fruitvale Station*, because that particular brand of American racial horror is still with us.

12 Years a Slave did indeed show the sheer inhumanity of slavery as practiced in the U. S., but it failed to show the life, love and intimacy of Solomon Northup and his family. I read Northup's account of his experience and I watched the PBS dramatization of his story aired in 1984. Both of these included a more complete picture of Northup's family and livelihood prior to his capture. I was disappointed to see that given short shrift in the later film.

I am pleased to see major American movies focus on this country's original sin. It is also a signal achievement that a major movie can finally admit that the Civil War, this country's most pivotal event, was fought over whether or not the U.S. would continue to hold humans in bondage. For a very long time the country has been in denial about that. Despite their flaws these popular movies, the latest of several **Hollywood attempts** to present that brutal experience on film, at least have the country talking about a critical subject that we usually avoid. The capture of, enslavement of, and commerce in the bodies of people of African descent went on for hundreds of years, and the fallout from that trauma continues to the present day. It will hound us and haunt us until we face it, talk about it and accept it as a tragic part of our history.

For a more complete picture of slavery read **"10 Things You Should Know About Slavery but Won't Learn at Django"** and watch the PBS American Experience series, *The Abolitionists*.

Links:

Tarantino's highest grossing film
    http://deadline.com/2013/01/django-unchained-becomes-quentin-tarantinos-highest-grossing-movie-406598/

this hilarious episode https://www.youtube.com/watch?v=DLD-HDUYkcA

Eric Foner http://www.nytimes.com/2012/11/27/opinion/lincolns-use-of-politics-for-noble-ends.html?_r=0

Hollywood attempts http://colorlines.com/archives/2013/01/slavery_in_film.html

"10 Things You Should Know About Slavery but Won't Learn at Django" http://colorlines.com/archives/2013/01/10_things_django_wont_tell_you_about_slavery.html?utm_source=dlvr.it&utm_medium=twitter

The Abolitionists http://video.pbs.org/video/2274405136/

Letting My Peaches Go!

Resentment is like taking poison and waiting for the other person to die.

~ Malachy McCourt

IN NINA SIMONE'S SONG, "Four Women," the last woman introduced says, "I'm awfully bitter these days because my parents were slaves." This line is followed by a defiant roar: "My name is Peaches!"

For a long time, I was "Peaches," consumed with anger and suspecting that everyone was trying to misuse me, especially white folks, but I didn't completely trust blacks either. I fantasized about how I would cut somebody to pieces with my tongue if they messed with me. Then I found opportunities to do so. That signature line from Simone's song is a capsule summary of who I was. It also capsulizes slavery's most debilitating legacy: the baggage of communal despair that haunts many African Americans. By holding onto despondent feelings we nurture the growth of resentment, anger and hostility.

My parents were not enslaved, but my great-grandparents were. My family, like many if not most families of African descent in the U.S., inherited frustration and bitterness from generations of living in a system designed to confine us in every way. Four centuries—sixteen generations—of being contained and denied led to a subconscious, hostile *acceptance* of the limitations imposed on us. We made cultural adaptations to help us cope with our antagonistic environment. With the help of compassionate others—Quakers who started the Underground Railroad and John Brown who instigated the Civil War—we fought hard and forced aside many of those restrictions. However, the vindictive cultural habits that developed through all those generations remain with many of us.

Most of the barriers we faced were erected by white power brokers. I repeat, *power brokers*. We often think and speak of whites as a solid group of oppressors, but in fact they are, like us, distinct individuals. Like us, whites don't all think and believe the same things. The majority of whites are scraping for survival just like we are. This observation does not diminish the reality that their struggle for survival may be made easier for them than it is for us. But so far as I can tell, many whites have benefitted very little, if at all, from not having dark skin. The absence of an impediment is unlikely to be noticed.

As I worked to shed my antipathy for all whites and opened myself to friendships with individual people, I learned that living with a black skin in the U.S. is *not the worst thing* that can happen to you. Over the years my white friends and I have shared stories of our childhoods, which are often similar, except that whites rarely, if ever, thought about race and racial discrimination. Some of them, however, have confided horror stories—sexual and physical abuse by their parents or other family members—that make my encounters with racism seem petty. The deep wounds of being brutalized as a child remain with them and appear to be more psychologically devastating than any of the racist confrontations I had. The racism I encounter is not, after all, directed at me personally, but rather is meant for all people of African ancestry. I have no doubt that pain and humiliation inflicted by those who should love and comfort you is the greater torment. No matter how frustrating it is to cope with racism, it can be mitigated by a loving and supportive family, which I had. Of course, anybody who lives in an abusive family situation *and* faces racism would be particularly vulnerable to self-destructive behavior.

Like many blacks I didn't notice that the lives of most whites were no more fruitful than ours. Instead, for much of my life

I cultivated a hatred of whites as a group because "they" were responsible for limiting us. And the evidence of our confinement was visible in nearly every aspect of our daily lives. There were places we couldn't live, couldn't go, or couldn't work, no matter how much money or education we had. Yet I knew that any white person—educated, moneyed or not—could do the things we couldn't. So I hated them all, even the ones who didn't make the rules, because they were happily taking advantage of their privileges. (Would anybody do otherwise?) I knew whites with whom my family were friendly who were kind, yet I held onto my general resentment of whites. Hating and disparaging whites as often and loudly as possible is what we did with the pain of being treated like outcasts, of living with the consequences that we were considered less than they were. In my world whites were the undisputed enemy; until I was in my thirties I thought white lies were the really bad ones.

Although whites were the enemy, we worked hard to be like them and hoped to gain their approval and acceptance. It's a tricky and demoralizing thing trying to be like people you hate. James Baldwin put it this way: "It is a very grave matter to be forced to imitate a people . . . whose existence appears, mainly, to be made tolerable by their bottomless gratitude that they are not, thank heaven, *you*." The mythology in my community was that whites could do anything they wanted; I thought they were omnipotent.

The irony is that I grew up in a predominately white neighborhood where, had I not believed so firmly in the myths I absorbed, could have seen that most of our neighbors were no better off than we were. *The only power our neighbors had was the power we attributed to them* and that we could have withdrawn at any time. Instead, we agonized over their "whiteness" and over what "they" would not "let" us do.

Hatred can become a comfortable cocoon, snug, warm, familiar. Every defeat can, with righteous indignation, be blamed on white folks. That means whites determine our happiness and well-being. We cannot succeed because "they" won't let us. When you live in a country where "they" run everything, what to do? With this mind-set, there are apparently few choices. 1) One can fawn over whites; say what you know they want to hear. If they like you enough they may allow you to get ahead. Behind their backs, mock, belittle, and disparage them so other blacks will know you still despise whitey. 2) Another choice is to outsmart the enemy. Be so much better at what you do than whites are and somebody, somewhere, will recognize and reward your ability. 3) Refuse to have anything to do with whites. Avoid them insofar as possible. Do everything you can to interact only with blacks or other nonwhite people.

A fourth option is to focus on your own skills and abilities and do everything within *your power* to achieve your goals. Find a way around obstacles, no matter what color they are. This is what triumphant African Americans have done throughout our history. For examples, see the lives of Richard Allen, Benjamin Banneker, Mary McLeod Bethune, George Washington Carver, Johnnie Cochran, Frederick Douglass, W. E. B. DuBois, Fannie Lou Hamer, Zora Neale Hurston, Elizabeth Keckley, Reginald Lewis, Gordon Parks, Harriet Tubman, Madam C. J. Walker and Booker T. Washington. These remarkable people and countless others did not allow a lack of money, little or no formal educa-tion, or even enslavement to stop them from doing what they set out to do. By being open to and looking for possibilities, they didn't have time or the energy to focus on whites, except to figure a way around the ones blocking them. Some of these undefeated blacks actually were assisted by whites who ignored prevailing prejudices to help them. In the story of America, relationships between blacks and whites are as varied, intricate and compli-cated as hand-knit lace.

THE USES OF HATRED

Howard Thurman, the late theologian and mystic, wrote about hate in his book *Jesus and the Disinherited*. Thurman says, "There is a conspiracy of silence about hatred, its function and its meaning." He goes on to say that hatred often develops where people have contact with one another without warmth and genuineness—in other words without recognition of one another's humanity. Thurman says this kind of contact tends to express itself in active ill will. We may behave courteously and even smile, but internally we are sneering at or castigating this representative of the despised group. According to Thurman, hatred is customarily applied only to the attitude of the strong toward the weak, but this assumption, he says, is ridiculous. The weak, or disinherited, are *not merely victims.* Hatred in the mind of the oppressed comes from bitterness made possible by sustained resentment at the treatment they receive. It is defiance of, rather than compliance with, their environment's assessment of who they are. Their bitterness permits them to assert their right to exist. Thurman concludes: "Hatred makes a profound contribution to the life of the disinherited, because <u>it establishes [a] dimension of self-realization hammered out of the raw materials of injustice.</u>" [emphasis mine] He goes on to describe hatred as a "tremendous source of dynamic energy." The trick is to channel that dynamic energy into efforts that are life-sustaining rather than life-defeating.

Unfortunately, the thrill of feeling intense hatred is seductive and contagious; when given free rein it becomes uncontrollable. I recall the popularity and promise of the Black Muslims—the Nation of Islam—during the 1960s and 1970s. I came close to joining the group myself because I was enthralled by their complete disdain of whites. It was thrilling to hear Malcolm X deprecate and challenge whites *publicly*! I'd never heard a black person do that; it was terribly satisfying for those of us who felt forced to defer to white power. Being full of hate, however, can make one hateful. Hatefulness can possess the hater until s/he lacks the ability to make distinctions about the objects of his/her hatred. Hatefulness contaminates everything and everybody with whom the hater is involved, even those s/he supposedly cares about. The disciplined, well-trained Black Muslims who were reclaiming discarded lives and building institutions in neglected black communities, turned on one another. Although Malcolm's assassination shook us to our core and made international news, he was not the only member of the Nation of Islam to be destroyed as a result of internal strife. True, the Federal Bureau of Investigation (FBI) played a significant role by infiltrating the group and encouraging discord, but the FBI did not create the climate of hatred and distrust in which the Nation operated.

Sustained bitterness and resentment first destroy the spirit, then crush personal growth, and eventually annihilate beneficial possibilities. More than anything the hater becomes consumed by reasons to hate. The hater loses the ability to see productive opportunities and sees only the negatives, the obstacles in her/his environment. This way of looking at the world makes a person eager for any information that reinforces his/her hatred. One indication of this is the seemingly endless supply of negative stories that are passed around among African Americans and accepted as plausible because of our history and inherited baggage.

These "urban myths," distributed widely on the Internet, often involve white people and are passed on as valid accounts. In one amusing story a hapless white woman is terrified she's about to be mugged without realizing she's in the presence of black people who are rich and famous. More troubling to me is the circulation of emails that include a litany of disparaging descriptions of things African Americans have done. Some I recognize immediately as frauds. I knew the bitter poem denigrating black folk attributed to Maya Angelou was not the kind of material she writes. I was at first taken in by the "**Willie Lynch Letter**," although it seemed rather modern-sounding for something supposedly written in the eighteenth century. The fact the writer's name was "lynch" seemed beyond coincidence to me, but the letter was treated as credible. It was widely cited and even published in book form.

The Willie Lynch Letter, now **discredited by historians**, was allegedly written in 1712 by a man who was a slaveholder. In this letter he outlines the ways slave owners can control their slaves by dividing them against one another. This fake document was touted as an explanation of why contemporary African Americans are not a unified group. Apparently no consideration was given to the fact that no ethnic, racial, religious, military, or other collection of people is totally cohesive. Groups come together and present a united front when facing a common enemy, or when they are coerced into doing so. However, once the enemy has been dispersed or the coercion removed, the unanimity evaporates. African Americans were, in fact, unified in their opposition to racial segregation, although not always in agreement on how to achieve that end. As we pulled down the pillars of American apartheid, our "unity" began to crumble as well.

The most widespread and effective use of divide and conquer operates on nearly a daily basis by America's power brokers. They consistently pit one category of Americans—based on sexual orientation, race, religion, nationality, gender—against another to make certain the mass of exploited people never cohere and threaten the power of those in charge. There were no "white" people before newly-minted Americans created the term to unite former European enemies—the English and the French, for example—into a group with which they could batter the indigenous people and people brought from Africa, whether captive or at liberty. The country was run then, as it is now, by that small percent with wealth and power. To keep people distracted from recognizing that they were powerless and exploited, they told them they were at least better off than, and better than, those colored people.

Even if Willie Lynch had actually written such a letter, why would we use it to explain current circumstances? Without much effort we can look into our history and find evidence that many African Americans have spent the past four hundred years helping one another. That is particularly true for that list of extraordinary blacks mentioned previously. Why not circulate a document praising black success and determining what it is that propels people to succeed despite having lived, or presently living, with the same racism as the rest of us? To contend that Willie Lynch's letter prescribed a system that is still effective four centuries later is to let our bitterness and resentment attribute too much power to whites. It reveals our own feelings of impotence.

Another instance of hatred's penchant to find something negative in what most would consider positive circumstances was the 2011 Jalen Rose-produced *Fab Five* documentary telecast on the ESPN Sports Network. The documentary egregiously insulted Grant Hill. Rose and Hill are two brilliant and materially successful black men who were both outstanding basketball players. Each of them received an athletic scholarship to a prestigious university. Both also played professionally with the National Basketball Association (NBA). As I write this Hill has retired from the Los Angeles Clippers after 19 years in the NBA. Rose became a basketball analyst for ESPN in 2007 after 13 years in the NBA.

The documentary was about Rose's college team at the University of Michigan, dubbed the "Fab Five." The film showed Rose as a college player disparaging black players who attended Duke University—Hill's alma mater—saying, "I hated Duke and I hated everything Duke stood for. Schools like Duke don't recruit players like me. I felt like they only recruited black players that were Uncle Toms." Rose's teammate, Jimmy King, went even further, saying, "I thought Grant Hill was a bitch." These are interesting admissions considering that the "Fab Five" were never able to beat the Duke team of which Hill was a member. They were teenagers when they made those remarks, but in contemporary interviews, both Rose and King continued to exhibit antipathy for Duke and for blacks who play basketball at Duke. Watching King trying to justify calling black players who attend Duke "sellouts," was unfortunate and an example of how uncontrollable bitterness and resentment can be.

SURVIVING HATRED WITHOUT BECOMING HATEFUL

In hearing and reading about those blacks who busted through or stepped over and around the barriers erected for us, I wanted to know how they did it. I have read every biography and autobiography of these remarkable people I could, and I've reached some conclusions. Although they came from different parts of the country and a variety of circumstances—several had been enslaved, some had advanced degrees, others no formal education at all—what fascinated me were the qualities they shared. Each of them had an inviolable sense of their own worth and nothing anybody else said about them, or did to them, affected that self-possession. This impervious sense of self kept them going. No matter what stood in the way, they refused to give up. Many of them also had a deep belief in a Higher Power and spent time in prayer and reflection. The people who managed to overcome were not spared any of the deprivation and humiliation— rape, brutal beatings, hunger, fear, lack of shelter—many blacks have endured, yet they did not burn themselves out hating. They directed their resentment to productive ends. Apparently they understood Howard Thurman's insight that "Anyone who permits another to determine the quality of his *inner life* gives into the hands of the other the keys to his destiny." Successful people keep their own keys. The opinions of others did not penetrate their spirits to define who they were and how they felt. Each one controlled his/her own inner life. Each decided for themselves who they were and what they wanted to do, and acted on that. There was no time to delay and no point in restricting themselves based on what others thought of them or what others *might* do to them.

Like them, I now choose to be the one who decides how I perceive myself and my world. In fact, it's the only thing I can control. I have no authority over what happens outside me, but I can always determine *inside me* how I *receive* what happens outside. Prosperous people, like everyone else, continue to face challenges and issues in their lives. The difference between being plowed under by difficulties, or triumphing over them, is how you respond. Your response is initially an internal matter. After studying the lives of black achievers and doing my own inner work, I've opened my heart and now see those around me without anger. I know they cannot damage my spirit without my consent. I no longer see myself as I imagine others view me. What other people think of me is none of my business. All that matters is what I think of myself. I've chosen not to hate and without that burden I am free to love and be loved. I've let my Peaches go.

Links:

Howard Thurman http://www.pbs.org/thisfarbyfaith/people/howard_thurman.html

Willie Lynch Letter http://rev-elution.blogspot.com/2013/03/durham-resident-is-author-of-willie.html

discredited by historians http://historyhappenshere.org/node/7204

Rules for Women Who Can't Do Enough
For the Order of Sisters of Perpetual Motion

*No woman can control her destiny if she doesn't give
to herself as much as she gives of herself.*
~ **Suze Orman**

WHO ARE THE WOMEN WHO CAN'T DO ENOUGH? We women
have been trained to serve and protect better than the police
force. Sometimes officers of the law go off duty; we never do. If
idle hands are the devil's workshop, we mean to put the devil
out of business. Permanently. Members of The Order of Sisters
of Perpetual Motion operate on four levels—Super Woman in
Training, Junior League Super Woman, Major League Super
Woman and Champion Super Woman. I never made it to the
Champion level (largely because I wouldn't stay married), but I
was Major League for years.

For much of my life I've been a member in good standing
in The Order, but I'm resigning. It's a gradual, ongoing process,
but I am weaning myself from being all things to all people.
What I've discovered is that no matter how much I do, it is never
enough—either somebody wants more, or I'm not satisfied with
my own performance. In fact, members of The Order are rarely
completely satisfied with anything they've done.

THE FOUR LEVELS

Super Woman in Training is still in high school but already understands her role. She's on the honor roll, takes dance lessons, is
a member of the cheer-leading squad, is active in student coun-
cil, has a part-time job and keeps her room immaculate. She also
helps her mother and looks after her younger siblings.

Junior League Super Woman, thirtyish, may be married or single; no children. She has completed her education/training and is employed full-time. Dedicated to her work, she is competent and thorough. Her employer loves her and has discovered that no matter how poorly she is paid or how much she's disrespected, she continues to work hard. Although Jr. League regularly works 70-80 hours a week, she also volunteers with Big Sisters, her church and her sorority. She dresses fashionably and has a beautiful, spotless home. There may be cobwebs in the kitchen because she rarely cooks, unless she's entertaining. Then she makes B. Smith and M. Stewart look like amateurs.

Major League Super Woman, thirtyish, may be married or single, but *has a child or children*. Because she's a mom, she works away from home no more than 60 hours a week. In addition to dropping the children off at school/lessons/games/friends, attending school conferences, preparing regular meals and, (if s/he's still there) comforting and encouraging her spouse; she participates in many of the same activities as Jr. League. Major League Super Woman may maintain this routine for up to 25 years, depending on the number and ages of her children.

Champion Super Woman, fiftyish, married for decades and master of the Super Woman role. She's still a dedicated employee, but now the children are grown, so the volunteer work expands to also include the Girl Scouts, YWCA, two evenings a week at the food bank, teaching Sunday school and regularly visiting a nursing home. On weekends the grandchildren visit, and during summers they join her on vacation. She cooks high-fiber, low-fat gourmet meals to keep her spouse's cholesterol in check and is available at all hours to assist or counsel her children, her siblings, and her parents—any of whom may be living with her—on any problems they may have. She has so effectively pampered her spouse that s/he is convinced s/he is the most important person in the whole world. Her employer has finally promoted her after decades of devoted service, so now she has money to help the children. Because her spouse might object to how she uses the additional income, s/he may not know about the promotion and the extra money.

I am making steady progress toward leaving the Order altogether, but it remains difficult for me to be still and do absolutely nothing, unless I'm recovering from major surgery. Giving birth certainly didn't permit any down time; I was in the hospital exactly 24 hours, and anybody who's given birth knows I wasn't resting. The best solution I've come up with so far to halt my perpetual motion is to pamper myself. It's amazing how having a massage or a pedicure eases the guilty feeling I get from doing nothing.

I finally understand that *I can't give what I don't have* so it's important that I take care of myself before I try to take care of anyone else. Here are the rules I've devised to help with transitioning out of the Order. Although they are numbered, all the rules are of equal value.

RULE 1: Say "No, thank you," to the things you truly don't want to do.

I politely say "No, thank you" to those things I know from experience I don't enjoy, that may in fact be torturous for me. Initially it was difficult, especially when the invitation came from someone I really cared about. However, the more I do it, the easier it is. Dreading doing it is actually the worst part.

Practice casually saying "No, thank you" in the same firm tone you use to turn down that third cup of coffee. Or, if that seems too harsh, try saying, "Thank you so much for the invitation, but I already have other plans." If the person is nosy enough to ask for specifics, tell them the truth—you plan to watch a movie, wash your hair, or whatever. Or, create an air of mystery by saying, "I'm not at liberty to discuss it yet."

RULE 2: Be satisfied with your best effort whether others are or not.

I've learned to be satisfied with my best effort whether others are or not.

In other words, I've let myself off the self-criticism hook. Self-flagellation is perhaps Super Woman's Achilles heel. We spend hours getting dressed for a special occasion then enter the room fault-finding. "My hair just won't act right." "This dress makes me look fat, doesn't it?" "These shoes really don't match my purse; I hope nobody can tell." We spend days preparing a holiday meal and watch people stuffing themselves on it. Afterward we see a few greens left in the bowl and think, "I wonder why they didn't like my greens?"

The issue here is that we agonize about what others think of us when chances are they aren't giving us a thought. And even if "they" spend every waking moment assessing each move we make, does it matter? I read a statement in *Sacred Contracts*, a book by **Caroline Myss**, that was a wake-up slap in the face for me. "When you do not seek or need external approval, you are at your most powerful." This is worth repeating. "When you do not seek or need external approval, you are at your most powerful." I mulled this phrase over until it really sank in. Then I memorized it. I think of it often. It has literally changed my life; perhaps it will be useful to you as well.

RULE 3: Plan events where you are the one being served, massages, pedicures, spiritual retreats.

I regularly treat myself to a massage, pedicure, a long bubble bath with candles, or a spiritual retreat. Often I simply put my feet up to read or watch humorous television. I finally believe that I deserve pampering!

The first time I had a massage it was sort of by accident. I was traveling on business and checked into my hotel with time to spare before my first meeting. There was a flyer in my room about a special on a massage. I'm usually game for new experiences, so I made an appointment. For an hour a handsome and skilled masseuse worked the tension and kinks out of my muscles and tissues. It was the most sensually satisfying experience I'd ever had apart from expert lovemaking. But I decided it was something to be done only on special occasions. Feeling that good after making love was acceptable because I give pleasure while receiving it. However, with a massage I just lay there and experienced the joy; it felt self-indulgent and maybe a little sinful. I didn't have another one for a very long time.

Years later I had abdominal surgery. After my incision healed, my physician recommended that I get a scar-tissue massage twice a month for six months. The masseuse gave me a full-body massage since that's what I had to pay for. Ahhhhhh! By then I was able to accept the idea that I deserve to be pleasured as often as I want. I continue to have regular massages. Not only do I enjoy them, but massages have myriad health benefits.

We all deserve to be pampered; if for no other reason than *you can't give what you don't have.*

RULE 4: Let the children learn from their own mistakes because they cannot learn from yours.

It took several reminders from my son, but I finally got it: he has to learn from his mistakes the way I learned from mine. I am intimately familiar with the maternal desire to protect children from life's knocks and bruises, but it's just not possible. I had an image in my heart of my child inside a bubble that shielded him from all pain. Yet, intellectually, I knew that falling down and learning to get back up is what teaches and strengthens us. Did I really want to deny my child the ability to learn how to manage his own life?

It may be the most difficult thing you've ever done in your life, but do not mess with your adult children's life matriculation.

BEWARE of doing so much for your children that they never learn how to take care of themselves. The possibility is real that parents will not always be around, so support your children's independence; encourage them to be responsible for themselves.

Do not, I repeat, DO NOT tell your adult children what you think they are doing wrong. Your time to instruct and guide them was between birth and age eighteen, or more likely birth and age twelve. If they ask for advice, rather than advising them on what to do, share an example of how you handled a similar situation. Then say something like, "I know you'll figure out the best way to handle this." Or, my favorite, "Follow your heart." If/when whatever you've said is ignored, pretend you don't notice. (Could anybody tell you anything when you were that age?) Your children will learn from their mistakes just as you learned (are learning) from yours. If they are too thickheaded to learn from their mistakes, nothing you say will make a difference anyway.

The most important thing you can do for your adult children is have a life and interests that do not involve them. Why? Because they have their own lives and interests apart from you.

RULE 5: Reminder: It is none of your business what others (including mom, spouse and children) think of you.

I periodically have to remind myself that it is none of my business what others, especially those I care deeply about, think of me. I know from experience that this is more easily said than done. When you have spent your entire life finding fault with yourself and seeking to please others, you can't turn on a dime and suddenly not care. It takes a lot of internal work, and you may need assistance from a therapist or self-help books.

I've read tons of books, watched hours of PBS fund-raising specials and spent five years in therapy. I also look in the mirror every morning and say, "I love you. I want what is best for you," just in case I don't hear it from anybody else. Besides, who will love me more than I love myself? It works! I'm learning to love myself unconditionally and accept myself just as I am, flaws and all.

Nobody is perfect. When we're not pleased with ourselves, we tend to put others on pedestals because they appear to be "better" than we are. If you think you know someone who's perfect, what that means is that you don't know them very well. Once you learn to love yourself just as you are, there is a huge payoff. When you are comfortable in your own skin, you exude confidence. When you're confident, people enjoy your company a lot more than when you were constantly complaining and picking at yourself.

RULE 6: Sleep eight or more hours every night so that when you sit still, you can stay awake.

I usually sleep nine or ten hours every night; consequently, I am wide-awake at church, in meetings, at the movies, while visiting friends, or while meditating. I get flak about how much I sleep. When I was obsessed with what others thought of me, I tried to sleep less, but my body wasn't having it. With less sleep, I was susceptible to colds, couldn't stay awake during movies and was just generally tired all the time. When I was younger, I could get by on four or five hours of sleep; but no more. My long nights of sleep along with regular exercise and emotional clarity have resulted in my being healthier than I've ever been in my life.

Perhaps you are alert and have inexhaustible energy with less than eight hours sleep, but if you doze off every time you sit still, you're **sleep-deprived**.

RULE 7: Do something just for the sheer joy and fun of it whether it's practical or not.

So many times I've deprived myself of a wonderful experience because "I can't afford it," or "I've got too much to do," or "I don't have anything to wear." I've never been at a loss for coming up with reasons/excuses to talk myself out of doing things that I *really wanted* to do. Most often, though, I've had to overcome the fear of trying something new.

Of course the longer I live, the more funerals I attend, and as I've watched family and friends pass on; it's become clear to me that *this* is the only life I have. If I don't live it to the hilt, I don't get a do-over. So I started taking the time, spending the money, pushing past the fear, and GOING FOR IT!

That meant taking advantage of the opportunity for a summer visit to Aspen, Colorado (where I'd never been), when my son was performing at a comedy festival there. On the way I stopped at the Denver studio of an artist I'd long admired, the remarkable sculptor **Ed Dwight**. It meant not missing the original New York production of **Ntozake Shange**'s *For Colored Girls Who Have Considered Suicide When the Rainbow Is Enuf* or the Chicago premiere of a play based on Ralph Ellison's novel *Invisible Man*. It also meant spending the big bucks for five days at a spa when I got my first book advance and going para sailing in the Bahamas when I was 77 years old. I'm having the time of my life. And although I have kicked myself for passing on things I longed to do; I've never regretted doing anything for the sheer pleasure of it. No matter what it has cost in time or money, I still seem to have enough of both.

RULE 8: Let the man in your life do half the cooking, cleaning and laundry, unless he really is paralyzed.

In my youth I was trained, and obediently subscribed to the idea, that it was a woman's role to cook, clean up after and serve her father/brother/boyfriend/husband. I was never comfortable in a serving position because it implied that the person being served was somehow superior. I knew my brothers were not superior, and after I married, it became clear that my husband wasn't either. It took a while, but I finally overcame my early training and rebelled against what was traditionally seen as the "woman's role."

Perhaps rearing my son apart from his father made it easier to ignore the culturally entrenched male-female roles. I taught him to cook, clean the house and wash clothes. He enjoyed cooking, especially making desserts, which I'm no good at, so that became his assignment. We took turns doing the laundry, and of course, his room and bathroom were his responsibility. One of his girlfriends expressed surprise that he knew how to do laundry. I replied, "He didn't grow up with servants."

Letting go of the idea that women are meant to serve men will not only elevate your self-esteem, but will provide more time for self-pampering. Try it; you might like it.

RULE 9: Take time to grieve losses.

Grieve all your losses, including the loss of energy, strength, eyesight, and ovaries—not just deaths and children who've left home. Go into your room, to the park, wherever, and scream, cry, rail against the gods. You have every right.

Even though Daddy, Aunt Sue, Mama, and your dear departed husband wouldn't want you to "sit around feeling sorry for yourself," they are dead. Instead of trying to please their memory, do what is best for you—*grieve*! Wallow in the pain; don't smother it in non-stop activity. Ignoring the pain only makes it grow—sometimes into a mental or physical disease. Taking time (weeks, months, years) to grieve will not make you lazy and shiftless. Nor does it mean you're defective, but when something reminds you and the sadness comes, go with the feeling, don't deny or suppress it.

It took eleven years but I finally finished grieving my mother's death. The first two years after she died, I ignored my pain and wound up in the hospital with major surgery. That got my attention. From that point on, I went fully into the grieving process. Whenever I thought of Mama and felt like crying, I cried. I wrote letters to myself that I wished Mama had written, then immersed myself in the sadness that flooded me. I examined her life and our relationship until I fully understood and accepted how I felt about her. My health has improved as I have gotten older because I have learned how to grieve my losses and allowed myself to do so.

I grieve *all* my losses, even the ones that occurred decades ago. I remembered how sad I felt when I realized my son was growing up because I could no longer buy his clothes in the toddler department. That was a reminder that every stage of life has its losses. Although not of equal weight, every change is a loss. When I suppress my grief, it doesn't go anywhere; it just clogs my emotional drains until they back up and throw my body out of whack.

Moving away from a place where you have lived for years is not only a lot of work, it is an emotional trauma. Feel the pain. Say goodbye to your former home. Create a termination ritual. Do it alone or silently if what others think concerns you (see rule 2), but do it. The new house/city may be wonderful, but all experiences, good and bad, impact your soul and when they end, must be acknowledged.

A change in a friendship is a major loss that may be overlooked. We cry about the man who dumped us, but when our closest confidante moves across country, we often ignore the pain we're feeling because we're busy applauding her improved circumstances. Or there's the situation when a friend gets pissed off for some unknown reason and stops returning your calls. After being puzzled and hurt, you may feel your pride kick in and say "good riddance," but the pain of the loss hasn't gone anywhere. Acknowledge it. If you don't, it may lead to a series of "accidents"—spraining your ankle, backing the car into the garage door, losing your keys.

When we face losses and grieve changes, our ability to navigate our lives improves and it makes for better emotional and physical health.

RULE 10: Go fishing or otherwise sit still and do absolutely nothing.

It's not a sin. Don't even read a book. By fishing, I don't mean actually baiting a hook with a worm and putting it into the water. Do that if you want, but I'm talking about fishing for new ideas, trying out thoughts you've never had before. The only way to do this is by being still and quieting your mind. This is also called meditating. Some folks do it while taking a long walk; however, if you choose that method, you should leave home without the earphones. Watching television does not count as doing absolutely nothing. That's because only Super Women in Training actually *watch* television; all other super women "watch" television while cooking, doing laundry or falling asleep.

RULE 11: Laugh as often as possible.

I've always loved to laugh and I do it often; perhaps that's why my child became a comedian. I love people who have a sense of humor. If I'm feeling out of sorts, I look for something to laugh about. If I can't think of anything funny, I watch a comedy show or a comedic movie, or call up my son, who unfailingly makes me laugh.

Not only does a hearty laugh feel good, but it's good for you; laughter really is good medicine. Medical researchers have learned that humor helps patients relieve stress and heal. So laugh it up!

RULE 12 – Say "I love you" to yourself everyday.

Look in the mirror every morning and say, "I love you. I want what is best for you."

Hearing those words spoken sincerely lifts my spirits and I reap the benefits whether or not I ever hear it from anybody else. I suggested that a friend try this because she was down on herself and seemed stuck in a bad place. She told me she couldn't do it. I empathized with her because it was difficult for me when I first started. I was embarrassed and felt silly, but I persisted. I knew how much I longed to hear those words, and it occurred to me that if I couldn't say them to myself, why should I expect to hear them from anyone else? Now I do it with joy and a big smile.

The words of my favorite song, "**The Greatest Love of All**," are true. "Learning to love yourself is the greatest love of all."

Links:

Caroline Myss http://www.myss.com/

sleep-deprived http://www.end-your-sleep-deprivation.com/

Ed Dwight http://www.eddwight.com/

Ntozake Shange http://www.goodreads.com/book/show/58098.for_colored_girls_who_have_considered_suicide_when_the_rainbow_is_enuf

The Greatest Love of All http://www.azlyrics.com/lyrics/whitneyhouston/greatestloveofall.html

Speaking Out for Mass Transit

We don't all have the ability to sing out over a racing train,
but we do have the power to speak up—and out.

~ Anna Deavere Smith

I STARTED DRIVING WHEN I WAS fifteen. The first purchase I
made after graduating college and acquiring a job was a brand-
new automobile. It was a no-brainer. Owning a car was/is an "essential" American status symbol; it's what you do once you have
the means. Ellen Goodman, the Pulitzer Prize winning columnist said, "Normal is getting dressed in clothes that you buy for
work and driving through traffic in a car that you are still paying
for in order to get to the job that you need to pay for the clothes
and the car, and the house that you leave vacant all day so that
you can afford to live in it." Having your own wheels makes for
the independence to come and go as you please, that hallmark of
America's prized rugged individualism!

The last time I had a car, about twenty-five years ago, I
hardly drove it, but still it cost me $300 a month (probably $900
in today's currency). That $300 was for the car note, the insur-
ance, and the garage fee at my apartment complex. I was living in
Chicago at the time, where it was difficult to find a place to park,
and impossible to find reasonably priced parking. Insurance rates
were astronomical. I was also frustrated by bumper-to-bumper
traffic on the Dan Ryan or the Eisenhower, while the car over-
heated and burned gasoline as the El zipped by. When the lease
on the car expired I did not renew it; it was a lot cheaper, and
easier on my nerves, to ride public transportation. Eventually, it
occurred to me that it was a good thing to have one less car adding to traffic congestion and polluting the air.

Reviving the country's automobile industry is one of President Obama's proudest accomplishments. A revival that doesn't seem to be working all that well for **General Motors**. Remember the slogan "As General Motors goes, so goes America"? That may have been the case in the twentieth century, but here in the twenty-first, it would be a smarter long-term move to re-train some automobile workers to assemble digital products. Americans do not have that kind of patience, though; we want fast-track solutions no matter how intractable the problem.

We are (and should be) outraged by firearm deaths—31,672 in 2010—but we yawn at statistics about the number of **people killed by automobiles**; more than 30,000 a year for the last several years. Our highways and streets are figurative guns and cars their lethal bullets. However, in defense of automobiles, unlike guns, they are not designed to be killing machines, at least they haven't been since Ralph Nader wrote *Unsafe at Any Speed* in 1965.

If our elected officials passed a law *forcing* everyone to own a car, people would be outraged. Why? Partially at least because cars are a major expense that doesn't end with the purchase. All states require cars to have license plates, and the car's driver must have a license and liability insurance. Some states require *all licensed drivers* to purchase liability insurance whether they own a car or not. Other states levy an annual excise tax in addition to the substantial sales tax on the purchase of a car. Then there's the maintenance—regular oil changes and checkups, tire rotation, antifreeze, transmission fluid, etc. ad infinitum—and, the most persistent expense, gasoline to fuel the car. Owning a car has not been legislated, but it has effectively been *mandated* by public policies— policies undoubtedly driven by the hugely successful lobbying/marketing efforts of the automobile and oil industries. Many people take on the financial burden of car ownership because they *have little choice.* Many residential developments are exclusively for automobile owners. I know this because in such areas every house has a driveway, but there are no sidewalks or essential services —grocery stores, health care facilities, etc.— within a ten-mile radius, and children must be driven or bused to school.

Access to public transportation is also a civil rights issue.

There are places in this country where people are FORCED to take on the expense of some kind of car because there is no public transportation available, or what is available runs infrequently and/or does not fully cover the area. Lack of public transportation is a critical factor for the economy and employers as well. Those who cannot afford cars are often without reliable transportation to employment opportunities. In some cities, Indianapolis for example, the shortage of public transportation effectively bars people who cannot afford cars from some jobs. Often when people do have a job, the schedules and unreliability of city transit wreak havoc with their ability to be there every day and to arrive on time. This is a major disadvantage for the working poor. When municipalities are criticized for the lack of public transportation, their response often is, there are not enough people riding for us to invest in it. It's a Catch-22. People don't ride because the bus runs every two hours and is rarely on time, so they've been compelled to buy a car, get rides with friends, or use taxis and jitneys.

As a result of new voter ID laws, millions of people without a car and the required license to drive it may be deprived of their right to vote. Eleven percent of eligible voters lack the government-issued photo ID that ten states passed laws to require of voters. (Fortunately some of these desperate efforts to limit voting were **overturned in the courts**.) To obtain this mandated ID, these registered voters must travel to a government office. Yet *half a million citizens* will face obstacles in making this trip because they live more than ten miles from the government office, have limited access to mass transit and DO NOT HAVE A CAR.

Another indication of absolute disdain for pedestrians is that after a snowstorm, streets are immediately plowed clean for cars. No mention or attention is given to sidewalks covered with snow and ice or the high banks of plowed snow creating barriers for people who need to catch a bus or cross the plowed streets. Pedestrians are forced to walk in the streets; a situation made even more dangerous because the mounds of plowed snow make the streets narrower than usual. A less serious, but seriously annoying, example of discrimination against people without cars is that some business and professional offices make no provision for pedestrians. There are only parking lots and parking spaces; no sidewalks or paths for those who walk to the entrance from beyond the parking lot. The afterhours ATM at some bank branches are for cars only. Of course, people can walk up to the ATM, but they risk being hit by a car because to use the ATM, you have to stand in the driveway.

The rights of those, including older people, who choose not to own a car or who can't afford the ongoing expense of one, are ignored. Some of us older Americans may be able to afford cars, but simply don't want to drive! It's nerve-wracking, and there can be a point at which it is dangerous! Some of us would much prefer a brisk healthy walk to the grocery store, or to the corner to catch a bus or a train to do our shopping. Public transport can accommodate shopping carts as well as wheelchairs. We'd like the option of walking or taking a bus to the train station to go visit the grandchildren rather than dealing with highway traffic either speeding past or riding the rear bumper. The ultimate, and patently unfair, affront to those of us who don't have cars is that eighty percent (80%) of transportation money in this country is spent on highways; twenty percent (20%) on mass transit.

In places where mass transit is excellent, it is heavily used—cities like Chicago, New York, Washington, DC. In the San Francisco Bay Area, the city itself has ample public transit, and connecting the city to the rest of the Bay Area, there's BART (Bay Area Rapid Transit) and Caltrain. It is possible to live there comfortably without a car. Along the East Coast there is a functional rail system that efficiently moves people from one city to another. It runs regularly and people use it; however, with rare exceptions the oil/construction/highway/automobile lobbies have effectively shut down this possibility elsewhere in the country.

California residents voted for a high-speed intercity train in that populous state because it has apparently dawned on them that they can't keep adding a car for every person to their already maddening traffic congestion. However, **controversy and litigation** may interfere with the actual construction scheduled for completion in 2029. In 2012, Illinois, on the eve of an election, tested a short run of a proposed 110-mile-per hour train to run from Chicago to St. Louis. Mark Brown, writing in the ***Chicago Sun-Times,*** was skeptical of the outcome as a similar test run had been done ten years earlier. He said, "Such is the history of high-speed rail in the Midwest, which is really only catching back up to speeds that were commonly achieved by passenger trains in this country prior to World War II (when there were a lot fewer cars to get in the way.)" According to the **Illinois Department of Transportation** web site, work is continuing on the Chicago to St. Louis train corridor. A similar proposal for a high-speed train to operate between Chicago and Cincinnati through the state of Indiana was killed before it reached serious consideration. Indiana continues to invest in new highway construction.

Nearly *everybody* in the Midwest has a car, and when I say that I don't, many people immediately assume that I don't know how to drive. They cannot conceive of my being unwilling to make the sacrifices necessary to own a car. I seem odd, eccentric to them. Admittedly, not having a car is a major inconvenience in a culture designed for cars because it takes longer to go everywhere. When the weather is good, I walk to destinations because it's more direct and often takes less time. Being without a car in Bloomington, Indiana is particularly annoying because public transportation is limited within the town, and until recently there was no mass transit between here and anywhere else. For example, local transit doesn't operate between 6 pm Saturday and 6 am Monday. The car-less have no business going out on the weekends, I suppose. When I first moved here, the buses stopped running at 8 pm Monday through Friday, but that changed to 11 pm a few years ago. It's a real treat to be able to go out in the evening now without first finding a kind friend with a car. Fortunately, I do have several generous friends with cars; otherwise I'd be a weekend recluse. One of the reasons I often consider moving to a major metropolitan area is so I won't be dependent on the kindness of others to get out and about. On the other hand, I sometimes ask myself, "Why is it embarrassing to ask others for help? Why is being totally independent so prized?" I feel a rush of gratitude whenever I can help someone. Is it possible that others feel the same way?

Apparently, the younger generation hasn't inherited America's love of automobiles. According to a 2013 **New York Times** article, "There has been a large drop in the percentage of 16- to 39-year olds getting a [driver's] license, while older people are likely to retain their licenses as they age." I was pleased to see an article titled, "3 Ways Public Transportation Makes Life Better for Pretty Much Everyone" in the March 27, 2014 issue of **The Nation**. This article says that use of public transportation has increased 37.2 percent since 1995. If this trend continues, there will be pressure on officials to spend more of the country's transportation budget on mass transit. So, there may be hope for us after all.

Otherwise, if we continue to ignore the needs of those who don't have cars and to be obsessed with automobiles, the whole country will become like smog-covered Los Angeles with road-raged drivers in bumper-to-bumper traffic on endless highways. America's population is growing and aging, so it's time to change our priorities and beef up mass transit accordingly. Considering the many years of neglect, perhaps the fair approach would be to switch the numbers to eighty percent (80%) for mass transit and twenty percent (20%) for highways. I'd vote for that!

Links:

General Motors http://www.nytimes.com/2014/07/01/business/gm-announces-vast-expansion-of-its-recalls.html?emc=edit_na_20140630&nlid=59022613&_r=0

people killed by automobiles http://www.usatoday.com/story/news/nation/2013/01/09/guns-traffic-deaths-rates/1784595/

Unsafe at Any Speed http://www.bizjournalismhistory.org/1960_1965.htm

overturned in the courts http://www.thenation.com/blog/170287/courts-block-gop-voter-suppression-laws#

controversy and litigation http://www.latimes.com/local/la-me-bullet-train-battle-20140609-story.html#page=1

Chicago Sun-Times http://www.suntimes.com/news/brown/15855486-452/brown-high-speed-rail-demo-ride-doesnt-wow-but-still-sparks-hope.html

Illinois Department of Transportation http://www.idothsr.org/2010_const/

New York Times http://www.nytimes.com/2013/06/30/sunday-review/the-end-of-car-culture.html?pagewanted=all

The Nation http://www.thenation.com/blog/179026/3-ways-public-transportation-makes-life-better-pretty-much-everyone?utm_source=Sailthru&utm_medium=email&utm_term=email_nation&utm_campaign=Email%20Nation%20-%2020140327&newsletter=email_nation_thursday#

Economics and the Ecosystem: A Lament

Real tragedy is never resolved. It goes on hopelessly forever.
~ Chinua Achebe in *No Longer At Ease*

THE DICTIONARY DEFINITION OF economics is "the science that deals with the production, distribution, and consumption of goods and services, or the material welfare of humankind." Unfortunately this definition does not mention the multinational corporations/financial institutions that operate more for their own aggrandizement than to benefit others. The only "material welfare" many of these institutions are interested in is obviously their own. Too many of them destroy the natural environment in which they operate, apparently unaware of, or caring little for, the finite sources of their wealth. They are so short-sighted as to be unconcerned that their policies and practices are rapidly decimating the ranks of consumers affluent enough to purchase their goods and services.

I believe the concept of "private property," not money, is the root of all evil. The "ownership" of natural resources like people, land and the air above it, water, and oil are particularly suspect. The "owners" did not invent these resources. Why should they have sole possession of them simply because they, or their ancestors, claimed, often by theft or brute force, what they stumbled upon? Natural resources should benefit all humanity as needed, not be rationed for financial gain. It is this "ownership" as well as population growth, that has the provision of water in a snarl in **California** and other parts of the western U. S. In 2002 *Fortune* magazine stated, "Water promises to be to the 21st century what oil was to the 20th century: the precious commodity that determines the wealth of nations." How ridiculous is that? However, once the "free market" convinced us to pay for tap water in single-use containers, why not go all the way and control every drop of water people use? Now that we can't bring our own water bottles onto airplanes, have you noticed that water fountains have become rare in airports, but bottled water is sold everywhere? Will the air we breathe be monetized next? We need to *think* more about these things!

Hazel Henderson, author of the 1978 book *Creating Alternative Futures: The End of Economics*, doesn't believe economics is a science, and more than thirty years ago she described our current impasse. "Contemporary economists...have consistently avoided acknowledging the <u>value system</u> on which their models are based. In doing so, they tacitly accept the grossly imbalanced set of values which dominates our culture and is embodied in our social institutions.... <u>High rates of growth not only do little to ease urgent social and human problems but in many countries (including the U. S.) have been accompanied by increasing unemployment and a general deterioration of social conditions</u> [emphasis mine]." The irony here is that, if indeed, economics were a science it would *not* be defined or considered in ideological terms.

The late **John Kenneth Galbraith**, a Harvard professor who was often referred to as a "liberal" economist, believed that economics should not be defined ideologically. In *The Good Society: The Humane Agenda* (1997), he said, "There is in the present day no greater or more ardently argued error [than defining the economy ideologically].... [It] represents an escape from unwelcome thought—the substitution of broad and banal formula for specific decision in the particular case."

Our cherished "free-market" economy is not free in any sense of the word. If it were, there would be no need for the Federal Reserve Chairman to tinker with interest rates; the market would set them. After the financial implosion in 2007, **Alan Greenspan**, Chairman of the Federal Reserve Board for two decades, admitted that he was guessing much of the time. I suppose it's happenstance that seventy percent of his conjectures benefited his colleagues in financial institutions. Apparently, the consultants who are paid millions to advise pension funds on investments are also guessing. According to a **study by the University of Oxford**, their advice is "worthless." These are our so-called "market experts." If we actually had a "free" market there would be no need for the appeal to human weakness and fear via endless hawking of products across all media. New products would be announced and consumers so inclined would try them and spread the word about their effectiveness or lack thereof. This would produce a demand for products people wanted and could use. Then the manufacturers of those products would supply whatever the consumers demanded. This is not, of course, how it works. "Let the market decide" actually means it's okay to hike the price of a drug 5000%; to destroy the earth by gouging out its insides and indiscriminately spewing and spraying toxins so long as jobs are created, no matter how dangerous, and corporate profits are increased. Americans, and possibly all humans, are motivated more by ease and convenience, than by what is best for the planet.

THE COMMON GOOD

Despite American pride in our "work ethic," I am not sure how much effort we're willing to put into improving our society and the environment in which we live. At this point it seems that our hard work is aimed primarily at acquiring status, purchasing power and acclaim—in other words having MORE. Most of us have little interest in the work required to get our governments to install mass transportation so that, for the common good, we can give up our individual automobiles. It is our demand for gasoline to fuel more than 200 million automobiles (nearly a car for every adult) in the United States, and our willingness to pay ever-higher prices for gasoline that ultimately led to the ongoing tragedy of the 2010 oil gush that marred and perhaps permanently ruined the Gulf of Mexico. Not only do we demand oil for our cars, but we are building ever larger homes that require additional fuel to heat. National Public Radio reported in 2006 that American homes have expanded from an average size of 983 square feet in the 1950s to 1,500 square feet in 1970 to 2,349 square feet in 2004. More, larger, grander. We've gone from comfort to luxury to ostentation. What's next? Will anything ever be enough?

I also wonder about the disruption to the internal balance of this planet when a billion tons of coal are removed *annually* and nearly five million barrels of oil *daily*.

Thomas Moore, author of *Care of the Soul,* said, "Earth is not a platform for human life. It's a living being. We're not on it but part of it. Its health is our health." The Hopi prophesied that "If we dig precious things from the land, we will invite disaster." Perhaps that is why there has been an increase in the frequency of earthquakes, tsunamis, hurricanes, tornadoes and sink-holes, and the swings from torrential rains and floods to drought. According to **Michael Behar,** writing in *Mother Jones,* there is evidence that indiscriminate fracking (injecting water underground at high pressure to release gas and oil from rock) is causing disaster. Even if scientists are investigating this, what precedents do they have for comparison? Are we willing to risk the earth itself in order to feed our need to continually have more and more of everything? I agree with Hazel Henderson that our conception of economics "has enthroned some of our most unattractive predispositions: material acquisitiveness, competition, gluttony, pride, selfishness, shortsightedness, and greed."

These words of the sixteenth-century French essayist **Michel de Montaigne** are relevant today: "Each individual one of us contributes to the corrupting of our time: some contribute treachery, others (since they are powerful) injustice, irreligion, tyranny, cupidity, cruelty: the weaker ones bring stupidity, vanity, and idleness." De Montaigne lived in a monarchy. One would think his statement would be inapplicable to a democracy, but it's a perfect fit because we citizens have abdicated our responsibilities to hold elected officials accountable *to us*. De facto, we are allowing a monarchy to flourish, except this time corporations, rather than royal families, have the regal prerogatives.

If things are to get better, each of us must accept responsibility to be the change we want to see. Otherwise, this becomes a real tragedy with no end in sight.

Links:

California http://www.redding.com/opinion/who-owns-californias-water

Fortune http://archive.fortune.com/magazines/fortune/fortune_archive/ 2000/05/15/279789/index.htm

Hazel Henderson http://www.hazelhenderson.com/

John Kenneth Galbraith http://www.nytimes.com/2006/04/30/obituaries/30galbraith. html?pagewanted=all

Alan Greenspan http://www.nytimes.com/2008/10/24/business/economy/24panel. html

study by the University of Oxford http://dealbook.nytimes.com/2013/09/30/doubts-raised-on-value-of-investment-consultants-to-pensions/?_r=0

Michael Behar http://www.motherjones.com/environment/2013/03/does-fracking-cause-earthquakes-wastewater-dewatering

Michel de Montaigne http://plato.stanford.edu/entries/montaigne/

Shelby Steele: A Bound Man
(revision of a blog entry written January 12, 2008)

Dogma draws a circle round the mind.
~ George Moore

I DOUBT THERE IS ANYTHING a white supremacist loves more than hearing an African American derogatorily critiquing African Americans. Blacks who are willing to publicly excoriate the general African American populace are given wide media coverage. They are also regularly rewarded in other ways with high-profile positions and awards. Shelby Steele is a prime example of this practice. Steele apparently owes his prominence to his zeal for deprecating blacks. President George W. Bush was so impressed with Steele's "learned examination of race relations and cultural issues" that he presented him with the National Humanities Medal in 2004. Steele's "expertise" on race relations has also earned him a position as senior fellow at the Hoover Institution, which has been described as "influential in the American conservative and libertarian movements."

I watched **Bill Moyers Journal** in early 2008 when Steele came on to plug his book, *A Bound Man: Why We Are Excited about Obama and Why He Can't Win*. Steele opened his argument by saying that Obama has concealed who he really is. Because Americans don't know who Obama is, Steele said, it would be extremely difficult for him to become president of the United States. He comes to this conclusion despite the fact that Obama has written two books that provided more information about his personal life, experiences and positions than we usually have from a presidential candidate. I recommend that Steele read *Dreams from My Father* and *The Audacity of Hope*; perhaps they will help him understand who Obama is.

Steele's premise in *A Bound Man* is that black people fall into one of two categories: bargainers and challengers. He says that a "bargainer" gives whites the benefit of the doubt. These blacks, in some kind of "coded" message, say to whites, "I will not hold the shame of America's past against you, if you will not hold my race against me." Steele says that whites respond to this coded message with enormous gratitude, and that explains the immense popularity of "bargainers." He cites Oprah Winfrey and Bill Cosby as examples of bargainers. Whites, Steele says, can be with such people and not feel they will ever be charged with racism. These simplistic categories Steele has devised for well-known blacks do not, however, explain such instances as Cosby's insistence, over the network's objections, on including an anti-apartheid sign on the set of *The Cosby Show*. Nor does it explain the occasions *The Oprah Winfrey Show* presented programs examining racism. Winfrey also famously broke her own rule of remaining neutral in political campaigns to endorse and campaign for Barack Obama, the first black presidential nominee of a major party.

What Steele describes as "bargaining" is the way people of African descent managed to break racial barriers in this country. It's the "bargain" Jackie Robinson made with Branch Rickey, owner of the Brooklyn Dodgers. Rickey asked Robinson not to respond in any way to the abuse he would receive from people who did not want blacks to play major league baseball. Robinson was not happy about agreeing to do that, but he accepted the mandate in order *to demolish the racial barrier*.

On the other hand, Steele says, "challengers" presume that the institution, society, or person is racist until they prove otherwise by giving the challenger some concrete form of *racial preference*. Steele identifies these preferences as "affirmative action, diversity programs, opportunities of one kind or another."

Once the challenger has been given the racial preference, in turn "absolution" is given, according to Steele.

Jesse Jackson and Al Sharpton are Steele's examples of challengers. Steele says that what challengers do is "terrify whites" with the threat of being called racist. As a result of this threat, Steele believes, whites never tell blacks the truth about how they feel about them, and this leaves blacks living in a bubble not knowing the truth about themselves. This ridiculous pronouncement asserts that "the truth about blacks" must come from whites. Again, this simplistic description does not account for nuances or, more particularly, for the history of blacks in this country. I find it interesting that Steele made no reference to America's icon of "challengers," Martin Luther King Jr., possibly because examining King would have wrecked his premise. Most blacks are grateful for challengers; otherwise we might still be in chains, or, at best, barred from educational and employment opportunities that were opened to us only *after we mounted serious challenges.*

Shelby Steele's twisted reasoning shows how convoluted the effort is for someone who grew up on Chicago's black south side to make his observations conform to conservative Republican ideology. I don't expect he'll ever write a book about the shortcomings of whites because he has identified a lucrative niche analyzing American blacks and finding that we don't measure up to his delusive standards.

Steele, whose analysis is bound by his ideology, also failed as a prognosticator: Barack Obama has been elected President of the United States. Two times. And many whites, as usual, are *enthusiastically* telling blacks exactly what they think of us and of President Obama.

Link:

Bill Moyers Journal http://www.pbs.org/moyers/journal/01112008/profile2.html

The Wit to Win: Oprah and the POTUS, Pragmatic or Authentic?

He drew a circle that shut me out—
Heretic, rebel, a thing to flout.
But Love and I had the wit to win:
We drew a circle and took him in!
                              ~ Edwin Markham

OPRAH WINFREY AND I MOVED TO Chicago the same year—1984. She arrived a few months before I did and by the time I got there, my friend Betty Rowell was an ecstatic Oprah fan. She told me, "You've got to see this sister who has taken over Chicago!" I, too, was smitten by Oprah, partially because I identified with her as a black woman, but also I could tell that, like me, she was not entirely comfortable in her own skin. Unlike many high-profile folk, however, she didn't pretend she had it all together and I appreciated that. It has been gratifying to watch Oprah grow into an ease with herself over the years, and during that time I was inspired myself to do the work to become more comfortable with who I am. Some months after I arrived in Chicago, I called in and got a seat in the audience of the show, then produced at the ABC studios on State Street. At that time, Oprah was going into the audience with her microphone to get comments on the show's topic. The day I was there the subject was hysterectomies, and I was one of the audience members who commented. (I do not remember what I said.) After the show Oprah warmly greeted each audience member; kicking off her shoes before walking down the line to shake hands with us.

Oprah feels so much like somebody we know well, that everybody refers to her by her first name. Black people feel especially possessive of Oprah and have firm opinions about her. At first I was surprised that so many of their assessments were derogatory, but I've come to expect that now. On several occasions I've weighed in to defend Oprah, largely to point out that objections to her were subjective, but then everything is. Several folk said that Oprah loved white people too much. I didn't agree with that, but I wondered if she gave black people enough space and time on her show. Meanwhile, my admiration of Oprah swelled when she did a series of shows on spirituality. I had developed an interest in the metaphysical, and her programs introduced me to authors like Gary Zukav and Caroline Myss, whose books I still read.

Oh, what a night!

Presidential election night 2008. I will never forget my feelings of exhilaration and vindication that night.

I live in Indiana, where you can vote early, so I voted for Barack Obama several days before November 4, then flew to San Francisco to watch election returns with my son. I was as excited as a six-year-old waiting for Christmas. On Election Day I cooked as if it were a major holiday. My son invited friends over after the polls closed and they came with food and drink. We were planning a great celebration. As we sat around chatting and eating, the television was running softly in the background. No need to pay attention to it yet; this is going to be a long night with voting results dribbling in and the projected winner changing from minute to minute. Suddenly somebody called our attention to the screen and turned up the volume. The winner had been announced and it was only 8 p.m. on the west coast.

THE NEXT PRESIDENT OF THE UNITED STATES IS BARACK OBAMA! A guttural sound erupted spontaneously from me, rising higher until I was screaming and pumping my arms. WHOOEE! WE DID IT! I always believed Obama would win the election, but it had been a hard stony road. The news that he actually won was a tremendous relief. WE DID IT! Even my rock-solid Republican home state had voted for Obama. I had spent days going door-to-door canvassing voters. I'd also logged hours in the local campaign office typing voter info into the data-base, and WE DID IT! I know President Obama is not a magician, but still, like many blacks, I expected that things would be, well, *different*, with him in the White House. After all, he's one of US! WE DID IT!

When an African American ascends to a position of wide-spread fame, let alone power, we blacks feel as if a little bit of each of us has broken through that thicket of blockades that separate us from the promised land of The American Dream (not that we know exactly what that is). That's why I, along with many other black folk, have struggled with what is perceived as the "disloy-alty" of the two most powerful black people in America, and probably the world—Oprah and the POTUS. Our shared history as members of this country's most despised group has created a bond among us, especially when whites are observing and/or re-sisting our efforts. For example, I doubt that any whites cared that the men who shot John Kennedy and Ronald Reagan were white. But most blacks felt personally betrayed when black men killed Malcolm X. Alternately, we were relieved to learn that it was a white person who murdered Martin Luther King Jr. This kind of racial affinity intensifies when a black face appears in a high place, particularly a place where blacks have never been before.

The power of Oprah and the POTUS, of course, extends beyond the purview of black folk, and therein is the problem. When one of us is in an elevated position and has the capacity to influence those other (white) power brokers, we desperately hope s/he will remember to help the brothers and sisters out. What we *really* want is for blacks in power positions to give us *all* the prime seats at the table for a change, except for maybe a token white or two. After all, whites have been taking all the seats for their people f o r e v e r. In recent years they've sprinkled one or two of us in for "diversity," but what they decidedly don't need is one of *us* making opportunities for *them*.

So, it has been with increasing dismay that blacks have watched as Oprah created one white media star after another—Dr. Phil, Bob Greene, Nate Berkus, Suze Orman, etc. Aside from her best friend Gayle, has Oprah made any black person a star? True, a few black authors have benefited from her book club, some of whom—Toni Morrison, Maya Angelou, Edward P. Jones—were already well-known before Oprah tapped their books. A couple of other black writers, like most of the white ones, were lifted from obscurity to instant bestsellerdom by the Oprah Book Club wizardry. (Of course my real beef is that I sent Oprah every book I published and she didn't anoint a single one.)

President Obama had fifteen official Cabinet positions to fill and selected only *one* black, Eric Holder. For the six "cabinet-level" positions, he picked three African Americans. Altogether nine of the twenty-one cabinet positions are occupied by "people of color." (Actually, I prefer the term "obvious ethnics," coined by my son, comedian W. Kamau Bell.) What if the POTUS had filled twelve of those positions with obvious ethnics, six of them black? The country would not have gone up in flames; after all, the majority of Americans voted for Obama. And those who didn't vote for him disapprove of everything he does, no matter how "fair."

I do understand blacks grumbling about Oprah and the president, but putting aside disappointment about things like best-selling books and cabinet appointments, I want to examine what may actually be driving these two people I admire.

Keeping it real, Oprah could not have become a billionaire capable of giving away millions of dollars and building leadership academies without being a truly savvy businesswoman. Obviously, the majority of people in this country are of European descent (for now). Perhaps O and the POTUS are just being pragmatic. Oprah would definitely have had a much smaller television audience and less influence if she hadn't focused on topics of popular interest—health and weight, finances, self-improvement, hair/makeup/fashion and celebrities. I once heard her say that on the occasions when she delved into serious topics like racism or the abuse of women, her viewers quickly grabbed their remotes and switched channels. Furthermore, I can say with some confidence that many of Oprah's overwhelmingly white book club readers would have abandoned her long ago if her selections had been exclusively black authors. My guess is that more whites have read books by and about blacks because of Oprah's book club than in the entire prior history of this country. In fact, via her audiences and those readers, she undoubtedly set the stage for Barack Obama to become the first U.S. president of African descent.

As for Senator Obama: If his campaign slogan had been LET'S END RACIAL DISCRIMINATION NOW, we all know he would not have been elected president. Except for the finely tuned speech on race he gave during his run for the presidency, every time President Obama has looked kindly in the direction of a black person, there is such a media blitz and vehement outcry that he winds up backtracking as fast as he can. (The **Henry Louis Gates, Shirley Sherrod** and **Trayvon Martin** situations are but a few examples of this.) Yet despite the president's studied avoidance of "race" (read anything having to do with black folk), a sizable segment of the country, though thankfully not the majority, is just plain disgusted at having a black POTUS. And they're vociferous about it. The reward for their public antipathy has been tons of media coverage. I could speculate about why the media identifies with these groups, but I won't. From time to time, we blacks need to remind ourselves that had he not been elected, there wouldn't even be the *possibility* of President Obama doing anything for folk like us, not even appointing eight obvious ethnics.

For so long—going on 400 years, give or take a few—blacks in the U.S. had a common enemy, and that makes a group verrrrry cohesive. We blacks were all looking for the same thing—a path through the thicket; the opportunity to play on a level field. (In reality, leveling the field is impossible considering the fact that slaveholders were compensated for their "losses" after the Civil War, but we didn't get a damn thing for hundreds of years of unpaid labor. Not to mention that we were banned from the line when "free" land, taken from the Indians, was being passed out.) After the civil disobedience and rebellions of the Sixties when the barriers to our (at least token) participation in American life crumbled a bit, our racial solidarity began to disintegrate as well. To put it in really simple terms, as we went to school and worked with whites, we learned that not all of them fit the nasty, hateful images created in our lore. In fact, we discovered that many of them are actually just as poor and powerless as we are. Whites also learned that we aren't as dumb and lazy as they'd been told. In other words, a few of us came to know a few of them as individuals and vice versa. This is certainly not a widespread phenomenon, but it continues to grow, if only incrementally.

Despite general grumpiness among blacks about the behavior of "our" black icons, I've recently considered the possibility, even the probability, that Oprah and the POTUS are not *just* pragmatists. I'm thinking that their behavior actually reflects *who they are*; they are being authentic. As people engage in self-examination and learn who they are, they become comfortable with themselves. They find the courage to be authentically who they are, no matter who is looking. It reminds me of the statement by Marianne Williamson in *Return to Love*, "As we let our own light shine, we unconsciously give other people permission to do the same." When people are in the presence of authenticity, it resonates in a deep place within and they respond to it. And that's a human characteristic not bound by skin color.

Oprah loved the topics she presented. She can act—I saw *The Color Purple, Beloved* and *The Butler* —but I don't think she manufactured her enthusiasm for self-improvement or fashion. The details of Oprah's childhood are somewhat less well-known than the POTUS's; however, her life was not stable as a child—she lived with her grandmother, her mother, then her dad while she was growing up. And she was sexually abused. Because she spent the bulk of her early years in the segregated South, my guess is that most of her childhood was spent with black people. Undoubtedly she also experienced her fair share of racial discrimination, but she has mentioned a white teacher whose kindness inspired her. It seems safe to say that her childhood experiences could have helped her to conclude that good and bad people are distributed among both blacks and whites. Perhaps that's when she learned to assess people by something other than skin color.

Everything written about the POTUS—his own books, articles too numerous to count and books about him—indicates that he's long been interested in building consensus by understanding both sides of issues. We also need to remember that the family who raised him were white people *who were not wealthy* so he undoubtedly understands and empathizes with ordinary whites in a way that most black folk can't imagine.

So, it seems that criticizing Oprah and the POTUS for being "disloyal to the race" is thoughtless and possibly uninformed. Instead, I prefer to focus on being grateful for what they've accomplished. Oprah produced *Beloved*, possibly the most accurate depiction of the impact of slavery ever presented in a major movie, but we stayed away in droves. She also built a leadership academy in South Africa and honored black women with her Legends weekend, not to mention countless other ways in which she has helped blacks, not all of which have received news coverage. Also, the reality is Oprah can't make anybody a star. What Oprah has done is provide a showcase for would-be stars—as she did for Obama. Each person chooses whether or not to take advantage of the opportunity. Let's also remember that President Obama was able to pass legislation expanding health care after this country had been struggling for decades to do so. He has also reined in credit card companies and improved the student loan process. These new laws will be as much of a boon to blacks as to anyone else.

As we put Oprah and the POTUS under a microscope, we should not discount their individual experiences, or forget *who they are*. For each person's story, at bottom, is personal, and cannot be explained by their supposed membership in an externally defined group. To judge them in such a way means we are holding them to some arbitrary barometer of blackness. That's just as vicious as the irrational measures used to determine that African Americans as a group do not meet the white standard.

Links:

Henry Louis Gates http://www.nytimes.com/2009/07/23/us/23race.html?_r=0

Shirley Sherrod http://www.npr.org/2012/10/30/163950607/shirley-sherrod-stands-up-to-the-politics-of-fear

Trayvon Martin http://www.thedailybeast.com/articles/2013/07/15/america-s-regres-sion-under-obama-more-backlash-than-progress.html

Not All Black People Are Poor;
Not All Poor People Are Black

Emancipate yourselves from mental slavery; none but ourselves can free our minds.

~ Bob Marley, from "Redemption Song"

When I wrote my memoir, *The Time and Place That Gave Me Life*, I mentioned being puzzled by people like Frederick Douglass, born into slavery, and Mary McLeod Bethune, born shortly after slavery was abolished. The oppression of black people at that time was virulent, yet both of them accomplished extraordinary things. I wrote, "These people and many others, *in spite of rampant racism,* had somehow broken through those barriers to participate in activities that had been reserved for whites only. I wanted to know *why.* How could some blacks … get past *racism* to achieve greatness when most of us weren't able to?"

I recently had a life-altering epiphany that may answer that question, but for others to understand the impact it had on me, I need to set it up.

The Washington Post of September 28, 2011 stated, "Hispanics now make up the largest group of **children living in poverty**, *the first time in U.S. history that poor white kids have been outnumbered by poor children of another race* or ethnicity…." [emphasis mine]. Although I consider myself well-informed, I was taken aback at this statement. Like many other people, I had internalized the idea that the majority of poor people in this country are black.

It has been kept mighty quiet, but the fact is the majority of poor children in this country have always been white. What makes the *Washington Post* item newsworthy is that for the first time *ever*, poor children from another ethnic group outnumber poor white children. Politicians and the media have successfully painted the face of poverty black, despite the fact that people of African descent have *never* been the largest group of impoverished people in the U.S. Yet, this myth is accepted as fact by nearly everyone. In 2012 there were 46.5 million people living in poverty in this country. Among these, 18.9 million were non-Hispanic white, and 10.9 million were African American. **Not all poor people are black.**

White poverty is mentioned in passing, if at all, to indicate how it was overcome on the way to great achievement. Writer **Caitlin Flanagan** put it this way, "[A] life in entrenched poverty, [is] the kind that no one sentimentalizes, because to be poor and white … was to be so far on the wrong side of anything we hold as ennobling that we look away and leave it unaccounted for in an examination of someone who grew up to be a person of substance."

It has long been standard practice in the U.S. to allege that black people are ignorant, criminal and poor. These prevalent images are ingrained in the American psyche and support the myth that most, if not all, blacks are poor. When the television sit-com *The Cosby Show* presented the educated and affluent black Huxtable family in the 1980s, many people, including blacks, considered the show "unrealistic." The widespread belief that poverty is primarily a black condition was revealed in a poignant *Nightline* interview I saw many years ago. A young white single mother was describing her dire situation when the interviewer asked why she didn't apply for welfare. The young woman replied in all sincerity, "Welfare is just for black people."

Admittedly, the percentage of poor people in the black population (27.2%) is larger than the percentage of poor people in the white population (9.7%). For twelve generations while many whites were working and accumulating money and property to pass on to their children and grandchildren, blacks were being held as slaves. Black folk were undoubtedly working as hard, if not harder, than most whites, but they were not allowed to profit from their labor. When legal bondage ended after three hundred years, the caste system of racial oppression and segregation continued to severely constrict the lives of black people for another hundred years.

An approximate analogy of those four hundred years would be having a specific group of people hit hard up side the head every time they ventured out of their confined area. The group soon learns to create a life within designated boundaries and not to leave the area. Then one day, the authorities who've been restricting them say, "It's okay, folks, you can go anywhere you want now." But the memory of being whacked whenever they'd tried to test the boundaries is painfully vivid. That memory stops many of them from leaving; they will never depart the comfort of the familiar, safe area. Some may want to risk it, but are discouraged by their loved ones and the fact that those policing their old borders sometimes "forget" and give them a whacking. The few hardy souls willing to take a chance that they will not be whacked, will be skittish the first few times they go forth. Even after making several trips without being whacked and deciding to settle in alien territory, they remain guarded. The memory of those long years of being whacked is never entirely erased; besides, they are reminded of the whackings when they visit or think of those left behind.

After hundreds of years of being held captive, then having our movements tightly restricted and our behavior interpreted malevolently, many blacks are just not interested in participating fully in "mainstream America." They do not trust the system that has whacked them for so long. Some have made a defiant choice to never imitate the whackers, nor to measure themselves by whacker standards. Other African Americans, however, despite the whacking, have been sufficiently resilient and resourceful to make a substantial place for themselves in this country, literally *from nothing*. To carve out that space these blacks had to battle smartly and persistently, insisting that America live up to its expressed ideals. By so doing these courageous Americans set an example that other oppressed groups have followed, and helped make this a better, though hardly perfect, country. Yet this monumental and on-going achievement is regularly overlooked in favor of constant reiteration of statistics reinforcing the myth that blacks don't measure up to whites and endless position papers on the dismal "state of black America."

I believe this constant emphasis on negative statistics cannot help but add to the misery of anyone who is already discouraged. One thing I know for sure is that I've never been inspired or encouraged by someone constantly griping about my shortcomings. What gets me going is being reminded of past successes; having skills pointed out that I have neglected to use. If you want someone to aspire to a better life, to take a risk, to get up after falling down, denigrating them and emphasizing their failures is not the way to make that happen.

Here's another shocking myth-buster: *Not all whites were slaveholders. Not all slaveholders were white.* My point here is that the vast majority of whites did *not* own slaves. Most whites were not and are not wealthy. The majority of whites, like the majority of blacks are part of the lower-earning "99%." Nor is the higher-earning 1% entirely white.

Slavery was **big business in the U.S.** for nearly three hundred years. Great fortunes were built on the backs of enslaved Africans. Some of our most prestigious financial and educational institutions were built with money from the Slave Trade; **Brown** and **Yale** universities have acknowledged their involvement in the Slave Trade. Old-money family fortunes, generated by the Slave Trade, have grown and been passed on to successive generations. **Native American Indians** occasionally had slaves, and a few blacks reaped the financial benefits of holding slaves. Edward P. Jones wrote a splendid novel, *The Known World*, about this rarity—extraordinary and determined blacks who managed to accumulate wealth and property in the antebellum era. Of course, blacks with money have been as subject to the whims of white supremacists as blacks without money. The destruction of **"Black Wall Street" in Tulsa, Oklahoma** is but one example. Very often these well-to-do blacks were unable to pass what they acquired on to their offspring because powerful whites either stole or destroyed what they had accumulated.

In a society where everything is measured by money; whose **citizens are thought of as consumers** rather than people, it is important to expose the falsity of these myths about all blacks being poor and all whites being well-off. These beliefs represent a deeper and more intractable problem: money is equated with power; being poor is seen as weakness. In reality, being powerless does not correlate with skin color. Our perception that money and color are linked drives much of our subconscious thinking and subsequently, our behavior. When a group of people are labeled as powerless, we interpret individual actions of members of the group as defensive or insubordinate. It's that assumption that encourages a tax-supported public agency to create a policy of "stop and frisk" and enforce it largely on the basis of skin color. On the other hand, nearly all behavior of those perceived as powerful is seen as predatory and aggressive.

I have long wrestled with the urge to demonize those with whom I disagree; to make them my enemy. This is especially pernicious in relationships with whites. In this country, with some exceptions, blacks and whites generally think of each other as groups of people, rather than as individuals. We ascribe negative characteristics to the other group and that influences our behavior with individuals. This has been my pattern and I have spent years examining it and seeking to rid myself of it. The epiphany I recently had vaulted me right out of this routine perception. I literally felt something shift internally. When I considered writing about it; I was apprehensive. My fear was that blacks, especially friends and family, will think I am betraying my people. To paraphrase the writer **Isabel Adonis**, "The hardest thing of all is giving up the privilege of innocence." There's an unclear line between recounting our history so that succeeding generations know where we've come from and clinging to pain so that it becomes our mantra. There is something forlorn about a person or group of people whose identity is a litany of suffering. We have to get past the pain so that we can follow the lead of the Douglasses and Bethunes and become triumphant.

So, if life begins at the edge of your comfort zone, here's to the beginning of my life. I've decided not to be like those people described by **Michele Norris** in *The Grace of Silence*, who "[cling] to festering, old grudges, the better to foster communal solidarity."

I attended a lecture by Dr. C. T. Burris at Indiana University's School of Public and Environmental Affairs on the "Causes & Consequences of the 'Evil' Label." The professor said, and I agree, that "evil" is a label applied to that which we see as morally inexplicable. He also said that this label is *subjective* and *interpretive*, and that applying the evil label may be mitigated by the evil-doer's *intention* and whether or not the act is seen as *justified*. For example, most Americans believe the 9/11 attack on the World Trade Center was evil because the perpetrators *intended* to kill people. We generally do not interpret the American invasions of Iraq and Afghanistan as evil because those attacks are viewed as *justified* in self-defense or retaliation in the "War on Terror." The fact that the U.S. has killed thousands of people who had absolutely nothing to do with the 9/11 attack, is also not interpreted by us as evil because those deaths are collateral damage, i.e. *unintentional.*

The professor further stated that we sometimes apply the evil label to whole groups of people. When that happens, whatever they do is interpreted as evil. Since 9/11 Muslims, Arabs, Middle Easterners and people who are mistaken for members of these groups (Sikhs wearing turbans, for example) are seen as potential terrorists; consequently *anything* **one of them does** is likely to be interpreted as evil.

As I listened to the lecture, my heart leapt the barrier of my comfort zone with a new idea. Perhaps so many whites see the Holocaust as more evil than the Transatlantic Slave Trade because the Nazis *intended* to wipe Jews from the face of the earth, but the Slavers did not *intend* genocide for Africans, but rather enrichment for themselves by forcing Africans to work without pay. Possibly the reason little is made of the fact that ten times more Africans were killed during the Slave Trade than Jews were killed in the Holocaust is because the Slave Trade deaths are interpreted as collateral damage.

Before that deeply emotional possibility entered my mind, I considered whites who saw the Holocaust as more evil than the Slave Trade as irredeemably racist. In that moment, I stepped outside myself and was able to view these circumstances from another perspective. I was shocked by this possibility; it had never occurred to me that their point of view was anything other than malevolent and anti-black. And, of course, that may be the case for some who hold that view. However, I suddenly realized I had been giving lip service to the idea that we are all the same, all human, different only in the color of our skin, but I had never *felt* it, *believed* it. In that moment I escaped the malignancy of this country's racial paradigm, in which we are all immersed, and was able to see the people I have spent much of my life resenting as fellow humans, subject to the usual human frailties.

I had subconsciously been ascribing *power and intentionality to whites*. In other words, I assumed that *all whites* are well-informed and capable of understanding human complexity rather than operating on myths and banalities. That meant I was probably also carrying the subconscious opposite belief about blacks, *i.e.*, that we are powerless. If I perceive blacks, including myself, as powerless, and believe that whites are all-knowing and all-powerful, I give up the ability to orchestrate my life.

Douglass, Bethune and other historic figures, as well as contemporaries like the recently departed Maya Angelou, Beyoncé, Berry Gordy, LeBron James, Magic Johnson, Spike Lee, Toni Morrison, President Obama, Colin Powell, Shonda Rhimes, Condoleezza Rice, Oprah Winfrey and countless other blacks obviously embrace their power and use it. By doing so, they become blazing examples showing that all circumstances, no matter how difficult, may be transcended. Rather than constantly reiterating black "deficiencies," we should explore how and why these people are not swayed or intimidated by the prevailing myths. Their attitudes and strategies should be studied, discussed and codified, if possible, so they can be disseminated.

For some blacks born after 1960, as was President Obama, being barred and restricted because of skin color has not been a part of their experience, so they are more self-possessed and see fewer or perhaps no limits on what they can do. My son, Kamau, born in the seventies, has that kind of ease. Unfortunately, this level of comfort is misread by many blacks as not being "authentically" black, or as "acting white." It is actually simple self-confidence; the look and behavior of people who define themselves without constraints. African Americans who hold onto self-defeating myths don't recognize self-confidence in other blacks, particularly when they see it displayed *in the presence of whites*. Those ambitious blacks who leave their homeland to immigrate to the U.S. from the Caribbean and the African continent are similarly self-possessed. Interestingly, they routinely out-perform most American-born blacks academically.

Undoubtedly, hundreds of years of being "whacked" or being a whacker have taken a psychic toll on both African and European Americans. Evidence of that psychic toll is seen in a couple of trivial incidents involving **Gabby Douglas** and **Tamron Hall** and their hair. Although Douglas was making history at the 2012 Olympics, social media was consumed with the appearance of her hair. Hall, an NBC news anchor, became news in 2014 because she did not straighten her hair before going on-camera.

Many whites, of course, believe they are entitled to be in charge of whatever African-Americans do and how it's done. (See the U.S. Congress and President Obama.) Blacks, who have internalized systemic racism, want to have their insecurities confirmed. Consequently, they insist that other blacks conform to their ideas of what is correct. These incidents were not about hair, but were about controlling behavior.

Fortunately, we have numerous examples that psychic damage is reversible. We can be transformed. It seems to me that our focus now must be on finding ways to do just that. **Gwen Ifill** put it succinctly, "Getting to define oneself can be the ultimate victory. But to fully appreciate that win, we first have to acknowledge the limitations we have placed on ourselves."

I have taken that first step to free my mind.

Links:

The Time and Place That Gave Me Life http://www.janetcheathambell.com/

children living in poverty http://www.washingtonpost.com/local/hispanic-kids-the-largest-group-of-children-living-in-poverty/2011/09/28/gIQArfC54K_story.html?hpid=z5

Not all poor people are black. http://usnews.nbcnews.com/_news/2013/07/28/19738595-ap-4-in-5-americans-live-in-danger-of-falling-into-poverty-joblessness

Caitlin Flanagan http://www.theatlantic.com/magazine/archive/2009/09/sex-and-the-married-man/7622/ (

Native American Indians http://www.ucpress.edu/book.php?isbn=9780520250024

The Known World http://www.npr.org/templates/story/story.php?storyId=1476600

Tulsa Black Wall Street http://www.theroot.com/views/legacy-greenwood

big business, **Eric Williams** http://uncpress.unc.edu/browse/book_detail?title_id=641

citizens as consumers http://www.unity.org/free/redefiningOurRelationshipWith-Money.html

Isabel Adonis http://www.mixedracestudies.org/wordpress/?tag=isabel-adonis

Michele Norris http://michele-norris.com/

Yale's ties to slavery http://www.yaleslavery.org/

Brown U ties to slavery http://www.brown.edu/Research/Slavery_Justice/

one of them does... http://news.yahoo.com/muslim-woman-removed-southwest-plane-sue-141629333.html?bouchon=807%2Cca

Gabby Douglas http://www.huffingtonpost.com/2012/08/08/gabby-douglas-hair-debate_n_1756835.html

Tamron Hall http://www.curlynikki.com/2014/01/tamron-halls-natural-hair.html

Gwen Ifill http://www.washingtonpost.com/entertainment/books/book-review-whos-afraid-of-post-blackness-and-sister-citizen/2011/09/06/gIQAus159K_story_1.html

❧ INDEX ❧

A

abolitionists, 109, 110
The Abolitionists (television series), 110
abortion, 3-11
Academy Awards, 100, 102, 104, 106, 109
Achebe, Chinua, 45, 140 (quotation)
Adonis, Isabel, 161, 164
aging, 67-72, 138
Alexander, Eben, 75, 77
Amazon, 63, 64, 66
Angelou, Maya, 116, 151, 163
Anthony, Susan B., 90, 109
antifracking, xv
Antifragile: Things That Gain from Disorder (Taleb), viii
Asian Americans, 59, 97
Atlantic (magazine), 96
Aunt Jemima, 105
The Authors Guild, 63
automobiles, 133-139, 142

B

Baker & Taylor Books, 57- 60
Baldwin, James, 18, 65, 113
Banneker, Benjamin, 45, 114
BART (Bay Area Rapid Transit), 136
basketball, 118-119
Behar, Michael, 143, 144
Bell, W. Kamau, 25, 26, 27, 29, 30, 35, 37, 52, 53, 54, 61, 108, 151, 163, 180
Beloved (movie), 107, 154
Berkus, Nate, 151
Berry, Halle, 101
Bethune, Mary McLeod, 60, 114, 156, 161, 163
Beulah (television series), 105
Beyoncé, 163
bible, 37, 76

166

"The Big White Lie: America's Racial Paradigm," 92

Bill Moyers Journal, 145

Binford, Lew and Sally, 19

Black Family Reunion Cookbook, 60

Black Like Me (movie), 104, 106

Black Lives Matter, xvi

Black Muslims (see Nation of Islam)

Black Wall Street (Oklahoma), 160, 164

Blow, Charles, xiv, xvi

Bogle, Donald, 100

Bontemps, Arna, 46

books and publishing, vi, 13, 17, 18, 22, 40-66, 70, 82-85, 104, 126, 145, 149, 151, 152, 154

Boston, 42, 51-56, 81

A Bound Man: Why We Are Excited about Obama and Why He Can't Win (Steele), 145

Bowen, Governor Otis R., 29

Brooke, Edward, 22, 24

Brooklyn Dodgers, 146

Brown, Buck, 60

Brown, John, 90, 111

Brown, Les, 85

Brown, Mark, 137

Brown University, 159, 165

Buchanan, Patrick, 94, 96

Burris, C. T., 161

Bush, Barbara, 99, 100

Bush, President George W., xi, 145

Butler, Octavia E. (quotation), 51

The Butler (movie), 154

C

C. K., Louis, 65, 66

California, xv, 19, 26, 37, 92, 95, 137, 140, 144

California Fibershed, xv, xvi

Caltrain, 136

cancer, 25, 27-31, 85, 86

Carter, Rubin "Hurricane," 102

Carver, George Washington, 114

Catholic Church, 79, 83

"Causes and Consequences of the 'Evil' Label," 161

Central Michigan University, 17, 21, 22

Cheatham, Smith H., 32-39

Chicago, xv, 15, 51-60, 61, 81, 82, 87, 88, 99, 128, 133, 136, 137, 139, 147, 148

Chicago Sun-Times, 137, 139

Chinese, 95

"Choosing a Life in the Dark Age," 3

Chopra, Deepak, 12 (quotation), 28, 78, 85

Civil War, 110, 111, 153

Cochran, Johnnie, 114

The Color Purple (movie), 154

comfort, xii, xiii, 9, 12, 23, 40, 52, 68, 69, 77, 103, 104, 105, 106, 112, 113, 122, 127, 128,
    143, 148, 153, 158, 161, 162, 163

common good, xi, 142

compassion, 2, 77, 111

Congress of Racial Equality (CORE), 14-15, 22

Connolly, Cyril, 63 (quotation)

Cooper, Ablene, 103, 106

Cosby, Bill, 146, 157

The Cosby Show, 157

Creating Alternative Futures: The End of Economics (Henderson), 141

crowd funding, xv, xvi

Cullen, Countee, 46

D-E

The Dark Side of the Light Chasers (Ford), 85

death/loss, 25, 28, 30, 31, 39, 67-69, 75, 76, 82, 85, 129-130, 134, 161, 162

DeFrantz family, 36

dharma, 28-30

Django Unchained (movie), 101, 107-108

Donne, John, 26

Dossey, Larry, 86

Douglas, Gabby, 163-165

Douglass, Frederick, 32, 45, 109, 114, 156, 161, 163

DREAMers, xvi

dreams/premonitions, 67, 86-88

Dred Scott *v.* Sanford, 93, 98

Driving Miss Daisy (play, movie), 105

DuBois, W.E.B., 114

Duke University, 118-119

Dwight, Ed, 128,132

Dyer, Wayne, 84, 85

economics, x-xv, 92, 97, 107, 140-144
"Economics and the Ecosystem: A Lament," 140
Einstein, Albert, 2 (quotation)
Eisenhower (expressway), 133
El (elevated train), 133
Ellison, Ralph, 128
"Embracing Compassion," 2
Empedocles, 74 (quotation)
entrepreneur, xiv, xv
environment, x, 75, 77, 140, 142
ESPN (sports television network), 118
Evans, Clay, 81
Evans, Mari, 46
"Expanding Possibilities," 12

F

Fab Five (documentary film), 118
failure, x, xiii, 87, 159
Famous Black Quotations, 55-62
Farmer, James, 15, 22
Federal Bureau of Investigation, 116
Federal Reserve, xii, 141
"The Final Reservoir of Power," x
Flanagan, Caitlin, 25 (quotation), 157, 164
Flav, Flavor, 105
Flavor of Love (television series), 105
Foner, Eric, 109, 110
For Colored Girls Who Have Considered Suicide When the Rainbow Is Enuf (Shange), 128
"For Love of a Child: My Journey to Health," 25
Forbes (magazine), 92
Ford, Debbie, 85
Fortune (magazine), 140, 144
Foster, Alvin, 54, 56, 61
"Four Women" (song), 111
Fox, Sally, xv
Foxx, Jamie, 101
fracking, 143
Freeman, Lucille, 99
Freeman, Morgan, 101
Freedom Rides, 15, 24
Fruitvale Station (movie), 101, 109

G

Galbraith, John Kenneth, 141, 144
Galilei, Galileo, 90
Garvey, Marcus, 60
Gawain, Shakti, 84
Gandhi, Mohandas, 90
Gates, Henry Louis Jr., 152, 155, 180
General Motors, 134, 139
Gibran, Khalil, 90
Giffords, Gabby, 97
God/Higher Power/Om, 74-78, 82, 97, 119
Goldberg, Whoopi, 100
Gone With the Wind (movie), 100, 105
The Good Society: The Humane Agenda (Galbraith), 141
Gooding, Cuba, 101
Goodman, Ellen, 133
Google, 63
Gordy, Berry, 163
gospel music, 81-82, 83
Gossett, Louis, 101
The Grace of Silence (Norris), 161
Graves, Earl (*Black Enterprise*), 56
Great Depression, 34
"The Greatest Love of All" (song), 132
Greene, Bob, 151
grieving, 82, 92, 129, 130

H

Hall, Tamron, 163, 165
Halliburton's KBR, ix, xiv
Hamer, Fannie Lou, 114
happy life rules, 69-70
Harris-Perry, Melissa, 97, 98, 105
hate/anger, xv, 2, 111, 113, 115-120, 153
health, viii, 25-31, 36, 37, 67, 69, 79, 85, 125, 127, 130, 135, 136, 143, 152, 155
The Help (Stockett), 101, 103-106
"The Help, or Comforting Whites," 103
Henderson, Hazel, 141, 143, 144
Hill, Grant, 118

Hispanic Americans, 44, 45, 59, 95, 96, 97, 156, 157
Hollywood, 102, 108, 110
Hopi, 143
How to Know God (Chopra), 78
Hudson, Jennifer, 101
Hughes, Langston, 46
Hurston, Zora Neale, 46, 90, 114

I

Ifill, Gwen, 164
Illinois Department of Transportation, 137, 139
immigrants and immigration, xvi, 94, 95, 96, 163
"Immortality: Beyond Marble or Monuments," 89
Indiana, iv, 7, 29, 32-36, 39, 51, 76, 135, 137, 149
Indiana Department of Public Instruction, 29, 59
Indiana University, 7, 16, 31, 161
Indianapolis Recorder, 38
Indianapolis Star, 39
Indians (Native Americans), 44, 45, 59, 94, 153, 159, 164
inner life/intuition, 51, 84, 87, 88, 119
Internet, xiii, 2, 64, 66, 116
interracial marriage, 13
Invisible Man (Ellison), 128
Iraq War, xi, 161
Iroquois Constitution, 45

J

Jackson, Jesse, 147
Jackson, Samuel, 108
James, LeBron, 163
James, William, 84 (quotation)
Jefferson, Thomas, 45
Jesus, 75, 76, 78, 82, 83, 90, 115
Jesus and the Disinherited (Thurman), 115
Jews, 12, 14, 19-20, 55, 162
"John Henry," 39
Johnson, Lynn, 67 (quotation)
Johnson, Magic, 163
Jones, Edward P., 151, 159

Jones, Imara, 106 (quotation)
Jordan, Michael, x
Joyce, Frank, xiv

K-L

Kanellos, Nicholas, 59
Kapklein, Colleen, 61
Kapoor, Anish, 99 (quotation)
Keckley, Elizabeth, 114
Kennedy, President John, 150
King, Gayle, 151
King, Jimmy, 118
King, Martin Luther Jr., 90, 147, 150
The Known World (Jones), 151, 159
Ku Klux Klan, 33

Lee, Spike, 107, 163
legitimate rape, 4, 11, 95
"Letting My Peaches Go," 111
Lewis, C.S., 103 (quotation)
Lewis, Reginald, 114
Lincoln, President Abraham, 109
Lincoln (movie), 101, 108-109
"Living History: Movies About Slavery," 107
Living in the Light (Gawain), 84
Lloyd, Frank, 36
"Looking for God," 74
"Looking Forward with Aging Grace," 67
Los Angeles, 118, 138
love, 2, 12, 14, 25, 26, 29, 34, 37, 38, 54, 62, 64, 76, 77, 82-86, 109, 112, 120, 125-127, 131-132, 148
Love, Medicine and Miracles (Siegel), 29, 30, 31
Loving *v.* Virginia, 14

M

"Making Changes, Being Changed," 51
Malcolm X, 102, 115, 150
Mammy Monument, 105
Mandela, Nelson, 101

Markham, Edwin, 148 (quotation)
Marley, Bob, 156 (quotation)
marriage, 3, 5, 12-14, 18-21, 30, 80
Martin, Sallie, 81
Martin, Trayvon, 92, 93, 97, 152, 155
mass transit (*see* public transportation)
Matthews, Ameena, xv, xvi
McCourt, Malachy, 110 (quotation)
McDaniel, Hattie, 100
McGraw, Dr. Phil, 151
McKissick, Floyd, 22
McQueen, Steve, 101
Mexicans, 95, 96
Michigan, xiv, 14-23, 32, 59
Michigan, University of , 14, 24, 118
military, xi
Miller, Alice, 31
Mississippi, 44, 103, 108
Mobile, AL, 53
Momaday, N. Scott, 45
Montaigne, Michel de, 143, 144
Mo'Nique, 101
money, xv, 9, 11, 17, 20, 33, 35, 36, 41, 53, 54, 57, 58, 60, 61, 65, 77, 87, 89, 100, 113,
        114, 123, 128, 136, 140, 157, 159, 160
Moore, George, 145 (quotation)
Moore, Thomas, 143
Moral Mondays, xvi
Morgan, Richard, 56
Morrison, Toni, 45, 151, 163
Mother Jones (magazine), 143
movies, 80, 101, 107-110, 127
Myss, Caroline, 70, 124, 132, 149

N

Nader, Ralph, 134
The Nation (magazine), 97, 138, 139
Nation of Islam, 115-116
National Basketball Association (NBA), 118
National Public Radio (NPR), 143
net neutrality, xv, xvi

New York, xiv, 17, 55, 61, 63, 128, 136
nigger, 2, 107, 108
Nightline, 157
9/11 attack, 161
Norris, Michele, 161, 165
"Not All Black People are Poor; Not All Poor People are Black," 156
Northrup, Christiane, 85
Northup, Solomon, 109
Northwestern University football, xv
Nunez, Elizabeth, 59
Nyong'o, Lupita, 101

O-P

Obama, President Barack, x, 93, 94, 104, 106, 134, 145-155, 163, 164
Occupy movement, xv
The Oprah Winfrey Show, 85, 146
Orman, Suze, 121(quotation), 151
Oxford, University of, 142, 144

para sailing, 128
parenting, 5, 10, 11, 33, 53, 66, 70, 71, 76, 81, 82, 83, 84, 93, 112, 126
Parks, Gordon, 114
"Permission Granted" (Washington), 97
Pitts, M. Earle, 55, 57
Planned Parenthood, 4
Poitier, Sidney, 100
politics, x-xv, 4, 12, 22, 29-30, 51, 57, 65, 97, 98, 108, 146, 157
Powell, Colin, 163
power, x, xi, xiii, xvi, 20, 29, 35, 48, 63, 70, 74, 75, 76, 78, 83, 84, 92, 95, 97, 100, 102,
    109, 112-119, 124, 142, 143, 150, 153, 160, 162, 163
The Power of Premonitions (Dossey), 86
Pozner, Jennifer, 105
Precious (movie), 99-101, 104
pregnancy, 4-6, 8, 10, 11, 26, 30, 31
Proof of Heaven (Alexander), 75, 77
prisons, 96, 98
private property, 140
Public Enemy (rap musicians), 105
public transportation/mass transit, xii, 133-138, 142

publish-on-demand, 64
Publishers Weekly, 55, 57, 58, 59
Pulitzer Prize, 105, 133

Q-R

Quakers, x (quotation), 109, 111

Race: The Power of an Illusion (video), 92, 98
racial paradigm, 92, 96, 97, 162
racism, 50, 92, 93, 97, 112, 118, 146, 152, 156, 164
Rankin, Jeannette, 90
Ray, W. T., 29
Reagan, President Ronald, 150
Reality Bites Back: The Troubling Truth About Guilty Pleasure TV (Pozner), 105
religion/belief, xi, 12, 22, 74, 75, 79-83, 143
"Remembering Daddy," 32
Return to Love (Williamson), 153
Rhea, Art, 29
Rhimes, Shonda, 163
Rice, Condoleezza, 163
Rickey, Branch, 146
Ricks, Vinita, 55, 57, 98
Robeson, Paul, 60
Robinson, Jackie, 146
Robinson, Sara, 4
Roe *v.* Wade, 6
Rose, Jalen, 118-119
Rowell, Betty, 148
"Rules for Women Who Can't Do Enough," 121
Ryan, Dan (expressway), 133

S

Sabayt Publications, 55
Sacred Contracts (Myss), 70, 124
San Francisco, 44, 136, 149
Sanford, Florida, 92-93
Saxe, Art, 16-24
Schultz, Howard, xiii, xv
science, 77, 139, 141

The Science of Being Great (Wattles), 77
Scott Foresman & Company, 56
Seat of the Soul (Zukav), 85
Seven Spiritual Laws of Success (Chopra), 85
sex, 3, 5, 7, 9, 13, 14, 79, 112, 117, 154
Sexton, Anne, 32 (quotation)
The Shack (Young), 80
Shakespeare, William, 89 (quotation)
Shange, Ntozake, 128, 132
Sharpton, Al, 147
"Shelby Steele: A Bound Man," 145
Sherrod, Shirley, 152, 155
Siegel, Bernie, 29-31
Simone, Nina, 111
Simonton, Carl, 28
Sister Citizen: Shame, Stereotypes, and Black Women in America (Harris-Perry), 105
The Sky's the Limit (Dyer), 85
Slave Trade/slavery, 13, 32, 45, 95, 96, 98, 100, 101, 104, 107-110, 111, 114, 117, 119, 153, 154, 156, 158, 159, 162
Smith, Anna Deavere, 133 (quotation)
Smith, B. (Barbara), 122
Socrates, 90
Song of the South (movie), 105
Spanish-American War, 95
"Speaking Out for Mass Transit," 133
Spencer, Octavia, 101, 106
Spielberg, Steven, 108-109
spirituality, ix, 77, 79, 82, 84, 149
"Spirituality and Organized Religion," 79
Stanford University, 27
Stanton, Elizabeth Cady, 109
State of Emergency: The Third World Invasion and Conquest of America (Buchanan), 94
Steele, Shelby, 145-147
Stewart, M. (Martha), 122
Stockett, Kathryn, 103-104
Stumpf Brothers, 32, 33, 34, 35

T-U-V

Taleb, Nassim, x, xvi
Tarantino, Quentin, 107, 108, 110

176

Taylor, Susan (*Essence*), 56
Tea/Republican Party, 94, 147, 150
Teena, Brandon, 97
"10 Things You Should Know About Slavery and Won't Learn at Django," 110
Thurman, Howard, 48, 115, 119, 120
Thurmond, Strom, 13
The Time and Place That Gave Me Life, 31, 156, 164
Toms, Coons, Mulattoes, Mammies and Bucks (Bogle), 100
Treaty of Guadalupe Hidalgo, 95
Truth, Sojourner, 60
Tubman, Harriet, 90, 114
Tzu, Lao, 90
12 Years a Slave (movie), 108, 109

Uncle Ben, 105
Underground Railroad, 111
Unsafe at Any Speed (Nader), 134, 139
Urban League, 16
U. S. Congress, 105, 108, 164
U. S. Supreme Court, 14, 93
"Using My Consciousness," 84

"Victims of Comfort" (song), xii, xvi
"The Viewer's Involvement," 99
Vietnam War, xi, xv, 22
"Vindication of the Rights of Women," 45
violence/war, x, xi, xiii, xv, 22, 92, 95, 97, 107, 110, 111, 153, 161
Violence Interrupter, xv
voting rights, xiv, xvi, 94, 135, 149, 150

W

Walcott, Derek, 45
Walker, Madam C. J., 114
Walker, Margaret, 44
War on Terror, 161
Warner Books, 61-62
wars, xi, xiii
Washington, Booker T., 114
Washington, Denzel, 101, 102
Washington, D. C., 136

Washington, Don, 97, 98

Washington, Harold (Mayor of Chicago), 52, 57

Washington, Kerry, 107

The Washington Post, 156-157

Washington-Williams, Essie Mae, 13, 24

water, 140-141, 143

Wattles, Wallace, 77

West, Jessamyn, 3 (quotation)

white supremacists, 92, 160

whitey, 114

Whitaker, Forest, 101

Wideman, John Edgar, 92 (quotation), 96, 97, 98

Wilde, Oscar, 90

Williams, Sam, 54

Williamson, Marianne, 153

Willie Lynch Letter, 116-118

Winfrey, Oprah, 79 (quotation), 85, 146, 148-155, 163

"The Wit to Win: Pragmatic or Authentic?" 148

Wollenstonecraft, Mary, 45

women, 3-11, 13, 20, 30, 41, 42, 44, 45, 49, 54, 57, 68, 69, 75, 79, 92, 95, 104, 105, 106, 109, 111, 121-132, 152, 154

Women's National Loyal League, 109

Woodson, Carter G., 47

Wright, Jeremiah, 81

Wright, Richard, 46

writing, xii, 31, 38, 54, 63-66, 82, 83, 86, 160

"Writing for Myself and Hoping," 63

Y-Z

Yale University, 159

Yeats, William Butler, 45

YMCA, 29, 35, 36

Young, William Paul, 80

Zimmerman, George, 2, 97

Zukav, Gary, 85, 149

Books by Janet Cheatham Bell

Victory of the Spirit: Reflections on My Journey, 2011
Sabayt Publications, Bloomington, IN (also available as an e-book)

The Time and Place That Gave Me Life, 2007
Indiana University Press, Bloomington, IN (also available as an e-book)

Famous Black Quotations® on Birthdays, 2003
Andrews McMeel, Kansas City, MO

Famous Black Quotations® on Love, 2003
Andrews McMeel, Kansas City, MO

Till Victory Is Won: Famous Black Quotations® from the NAACP, 2002
Washington Square Press, Simon & Schuster, New York, NY
(also available as an e-book)

Famous Black Quotations® on Mothers, 2002
Andrews McMeel, Kansas City, MO

Famous Black Quotations® on Sisters, 2002
Andrews McMeel, Kansas City, MO

Stretch Your Wings: Famous Black Quotations® for Teens, 1999
(co-author) Little, Brown and Company, Boston, MA

The Soul of Success: Inspiring Quotations for Entrepreneurs, 1997
John Wiley & Sons, New York, NY

Victory of the Spirit: Meditations on Black Quotations, 1996
Warner Books (now Grand Central Publishing), New York, NY

Famous Black Quotations®, 1995
Warner Books, New York, NY

Famous Black Quotations® on Women, Love and other topics, 1992
Sabayt Publications, Chicago, IL

Famous Black Quotations® and Some Not So Famous, 1986
Sabayt Publications, Chicago, IL

ABOUT THE AUTHOR

Janet Cheatham Bell is an author, an editor, a recovering academic, a mom (to comedian W. Kamau Bell), and a grateful grandmother (to the smartest, funniest granddaughters ever... although she may be totally biased). At almost 80, she is still following her inclination to explore new opportunities and take risks.

At 47, Janet quit her corporate job to develop her own books. Her first, *Famous Black Quotations and some not so famous* was self-published in 1986. She licensed the rights of her first two titles to Warner Books. Warner combined the two in one volume, published in 1995. *Famous Black Quotations* was a bestseller, so other publishers wanted in. Within the next seven years Janet had nine books of quotations on the market. In 2013, she was cited on national television by Henry Louis Gates Jr. as "a pioneer in doing books of black quotations."

Janet most enjoys sharing her own thoughts and opinions. She first did this in a collection of one-page essays, *Victory of the Spirit: Meditations on Black Quotations*, published by Warner in 1996, updated and re-published in 2011 by Sabayt Publications as *Victory of the Spirit: Reflections on My Journey*. In 2007, Indiana University Press published her coming-of-age story, *The Time and Place That Gave Me Life*, which has been called "the best form of social history: a story that focuses on an ordinary individual but also illuminates the experiences of many over time."

www.janetcheathambell.com

ABOUT THE DESIGNER

Merridee LaMantia began attending the College of Design, Architecture and Art at the University of Cincinnati in 1968. During the 1970's, her love of architecture led her on many adventures which included the western United States, Mexico, Ireland, England and France before she settled in Boston, Massachusetts.

In the late 1970s, LaMantia's interests shifted to technical illustration and graphic design. This work soon led her to become the art director for the national monthly publication, *The East West Journal.*

In 1982, along with her husband and baby girl, she moved to south central Indiana to live near family and to continue her graphic design career. From a stint in the town's newspaper art department to nineteen years as a senior designer at an international educational association, she has designed everything from advertising to educational books. Throughout her career, LaMantia has maintained an active freelance design business which allows her the freedom to select projects in harmony with her philosophical viewpoint and also, collaborate with the many clients she seeks to support.

LaMantia appreciates the richness of a creative life that centers around infinite possibilities, family, three wonderful daughters, two sons-in-law, a new granddaughter and her loving husband (also an artist.)

This book produced by Belmantia Publishing Services

belmantiapublishing@gmail.com

Book and cover designer: Merridee LaMantia

Compositor: Merridee LaMantia

Typeface: Minion Pro and Myriad Pro

Made in the USA
Monee, IL
25 January 2022

89858316R00121